Give Me Back My Credit!

Denise Richardson

Copyright © 2006 by Denise Richardson

ISBN 0-7414-3474-1

Published by:

INFI∞ITY
PUBLISHING.COM
1094 New DeHaven Street, Suite 100
West Conshohocken, PA 19428-2713
Info@buybooksontheweb.com
www.buybooksontheweb.com
Toll-free (877) BUY BOOK
Local Phone (610) 941-9999
Fax (610) 941-9959

Printed in the United States of America

Printed on Recycled Paper

Published November 2006

Dedications

Michael –I couldn't have completed this book without your constant support, encouragement, devotion and unending faith in me. Finishing this project wouldn't have been possible without you in my life.

Mom, friends and family- Thank you for your patience, love and understanding –all which allowed me the freedom necessary to complete this project. To Jo –thanks for being there! Deb, Glenn, Mark & Judi –thank you for "getting" it all along!

To the countless consumers who have contacted me over the years – you have been a continual source of strength, insight and inspiration to me. May this book validate your personal experiences and empower you to help others to better understand your struggles and speak out for stronger consumer protection laws.

Thank you, Kate & James at Thompson Multi-Media. Kevin Peterson-thanks for that Aha moment!

Paul, Ed and Ira – Many thanks for your steadfast support and for your continuing efforts to protect and defend our consumer rights.

Infinity Publishing –Thank you for providing me with a voice! Alex, Chris and Michelle–thanks for responding to my many questions and emails with kindness and patience!

Give Me Back My Credit!

Table of Contents

Introduction

A number is a very concrete thing. It always represents a quantity, yet can also signify quality (a score of 9.7 out of 10), duration (since 1915), or time (8:30 a.m.). Numbers can also have mysterious, magical characteristics. Superstition whispers that 1 is a lonely number, 13 bodes ill-fortune, and a stitch in time saves 9. Every child knows that Snow White had seven dwarfs and the genie in the bottle grants exactly three wishes.

These examples of numbers being powerful, mystical forces are confined to the realm of myth and fairytale. However, there is a certain group of numbers that can hold the very key to the doors of your life. The numbers I am referring to are known universally as your credit score. The recipe used to come up with your score is a longstanding secret, mysteriously devised by Fair Isaac Corporation, and heavily utilized, by lenders and three large corporations, known worldwide as "The Credit Bureaus" or the "Credit Reporting Agencies," commonly referred to by the acronym "CRA." The three national credit bureaus are Experian, Trans Union, and Equifax, commonly known as "the big three."

I would like to begin this book, this story of my inability to obtain and hold on to an accurate credit identity, with a simple explanation of this not-so-simplistic number. A credit score is a consumer's permanent record that fluctuates according to what that consumer's report contains at any given period. Creditors (also known as furnishers) supply data to the credit bureaus, reporting monthly on just how financially responsible you are. These reports will not take into account any health problems, job loss, natural disaster or catastrophe. No, it doesn't leave room for those pesky everyday occurrences that could explain or excuse a late payment. Oh, no. Rather, a credit report sticks right to the point. Does a certain consumer pay on time, been late, how late? How much debt does he have, where does he work, where does he live, how much available credit does he have and who are his creditors? There is no veering from that path for loss of employment, home or health due to any loss, hurricanes, tornados, etc.—this is reporting of strictly the facts! But, I should note that these facts are often pure fiction, containing myths caused by identity theft or inaccurate reporting. It may, and usually does, take years to correct such mistakes. This score is also directly related to how much interest a consumer will pay on a loan or how high insurance premiums will be. A credit report can even affect possibilities for career advancement or a new job.

In a move that allows even more complexity, the CRAs have recently announced that though most lenders utilize Fair Isaac's FICO scoring model, the credit agencies have created their own secretive model that will become known as your "vantage score." In addition, these agencies have decided that they will now turn this mysterious three digit code into an actual grade. Think of it as quite similar to the report card we were once required to give our parents. In that day, our teachers compiled our test scores, class participation, and general skills in order to convert the total into a grade. Just as in school, our credit "grades" reflect creditworthiness with an A,B,C,D, or F, except this time that last letter's significance extends beyond the fearsome figure of our parents. This grade carries with it great weight that will determine what choices we have, or don't have, available to us. It affects the most important aspects of our lives, including the home where we eat dinner with our families or the car we use to drive to work.

Whether it is called a FICO score, credit score, a vantage score or a grade, your credit score is derived at by using a top-secret recipe to which no consumer is privy. Most creditors and many auto and home insurers determine your rates and fees only from that score, without actually seeing your entire credit file. Many factors are considered in the recipe for your score, some of which include: "Lack of recent bank revolving information," "Time since delinquency is too recent or unknown," or "Proportion of balances to credit limits is too high on bank revolving or other revolving accounts." Sometimes—actually, the statistics prove that more often than not—bogus information supplied to the CRAs by creditors is inserted into our files without our knowledge and is then utilized in the secret recipe to compute our scores. The scores are based on the data in your credit file at the time the score is obtained. Therefore, as soon as <u>any</u> data in your file changes, such as a creditor updating your account with a new balance, your score changes too, making it all the more difficult for an average consumer to stay on top of.

If the process of understanding and managing your credit rating seems complicated to you, there's a good reason—it is! In fact, until consumer groups screamed loud enough for our right to know what our score was, consumers weren't allowed to obtain their score—not until 2001. Only creditors had access to it, using your credit grades to make their decisions on how much credit to allow you and at what rate of interest, keeping the consumer completely in the dark. At least in school we never failed to receive our grades for free every semester. We had the results in advance and knew what reward or punishment we were in for. Now, we must purchase that score if we wish to monitor if and why our "rating" is fluctuating. Consumers often have no way of knowing what they are being graded on and whether the recipe used to obtain that score is based on accurate information. Thanks in part to consumer advocacy groups and the State of California leading the way we are now allowed to know what our once elusive score is.

Through the Fair Credit Reporting Act (FCRA) and amendments contained in the Fair and Accurate Credit Transaction Act of 2003 (a/k/a FACT ACT or FACTA) federal law provided for a consumer's right to obtain a free copy of his credit report annually from each of the "big three." The only way to get that free report is through a centralized source, a combined effort by the three national bureaus. The annual free reports are available through a dedicated web site, AnnualCreditReport.com. BUT BEWARE!

American Consumer Credit Education Support Services (ACCESS) has issued a consumer warning about the website AnnualCreditReport.com. The site's privacy policy is not consumer friendly.

The AnnualCreditReport.com website was set up in a partnership between Experian, Equifax and Trans Union to provide free credit reports to consumers on an annual basis. The site was created in response to the Fair and Accurate Credit Transactions Act (FACT Act), passed by Congress in late 2003, which gives consumers the right to get one free credit report annually from each of the three credit repositories. Congress' intent with the FACT Act was to give consumers the ability to review the data appearing in their credit file.

Unfortunately, the repositories have elected to incorporate language into the site's privacy policy which allows them to share, sell, and reuse the data that consumers provide them while using the site. Sharing of such data, which includes Social Security Number, can cause identity theft, credit card fraud, and other financial problems, the very things Congress is trying to remedy.

"This activity is merely another attempt by the big 3 national CRAs to move our personal and confidential credit information into the hands of marketers," stated L.E. Tighe, ACCESS founder and board member. "The 2003 amendments to the FCRA allow affiliate sharing, however, this information is to be clearly and conspicuously disclosed to the consumer. They are also to provide the consumer a simple method to prohibit the sharing of their information."

"If the big 3 CRAs are going to provide credit reports online," Tighe continued, "they should comply with the spirit and letter of the law by allowing consumers to easily opt-out. With something as personal and confidential as a credit report, we believe a simple pop-up window alerting the consumer of affiliate sharing, while providing a simple yes/no response on whether the consumer wishes this to occur, is not out of line."

On the ACCESS website (guardmycreditfile.org) they advise consumers interested in exercising their rights under the FACT Act, to make their credit report request via the telephone instead of using the website. The number to call is **877-322-8228**. The number is toll free and there is a pre-recorded statement which guarantees that your personal data will only be used for the purpose of providing their credit report.

If you want to call a CRA to discuss your report or score—forget it. You will have to have already ordered and received your consumer report directly from that CRA instead of one of the many "resellers" (someone under contract with the "big three") allowed to sell credit reports online to consumers. All CRAs utilize automation, requiring the input of the actual report number contained in the credit report in question. If you do not have this number, you can't speak with a human being. Under FACTA provisions, consumers have a right to their credit report—the report, but not the score. You will not receive that all-important three digit number in the free report. Consumers must request a credit score including an explanation of the factors that went into computing the score—and pay for that. Translation: you will get your score (for a price) but never the exact recipe used to derive your score.

The free annual concession actually works in the credit agencies' favor because as identity theft continues to explode, so does the number of credit reports purchased beyond the free annual copy. Additionally, the CRAs now sell their own "monitoring services" wherein they promise (for a fee) to monitor your credit report and notify you if any adverse action has been taken while allowing you more frequent access to your credit reports. Public Interest Research Group (PIRG) Consumer Tip: watch out. The bureaus will try to convince you to pay $40, $50 or $100 or more for various other credit monitoring services. PIRG thinks these are unnecessary. Get your free report, as provided by law, and consider getting a reasonably priced credit score (likely $5-8 dollars), but don't pay extra to enrich the credit bureaus. With more and more consumers being afflicted with fraud and frightened at the mere thought of identity theft wreaking havoc in their lives, more and more will pay for unnecessary services that obviously make the credit bureaus' profits soar and leaves them with much more work to do in perfecting the information they disseminate, data that they often don't care is erroneous. If you are intent on purchasing a monitoring system, beware of the monitoring services offered by most credit card companies as they usually only offer to monitor one credit reporting agency –not all of them. I would check out Life Lock, a company based in Arizona that claims to provide free services to hurricane victims, tornado victims, and veterans. Life Lock offers to set fraud alerts on all of your credit reports and renew the alerts continually so they never "fall off" your reports. They also claim to guarantee that if you become a victim of identity theft while you are their client – they will fix it and reimburse you for any out-of pocket expenses you incur, up to $1,000,000.00. Consumers in a sense, work as unpaid employees of the credit bureaus. They are fact-checkers of mistakes, continually writing dispute letters trying to replace fiction with truth. In essence, consumers are doing the CRA's work for them; being the true investigators and providers of the information the CRAs sell—to us!

Many consumers, unaware of their credit report's discrepancies, are also unaware of the obstacles consumers face when seeking to correct costly and dangerous errors once they are disseminated to potential creditors. Consumer protection laws intended to safeguard consumers from abusive or inaccurate credit reporting, are complex, weak and riddled with loopholes. Creditors and the CRAs often twist the intent of these laws and use them as sword against consumers, stripping away the intent -and our rights.

According to Edmund Mierzwinski, the Consumer Program Director of the U.S. P.I.R.G. (United States Public Interest Research Group) and author of numerous reports on credit cards and the credit reporting industry, explains what the FCRA is supposed to do in laymen's terms: "The amended Fair Credit Reporting Act says: Prevent identity theft! Give consumers the right to a free credit report! Regulate the industry to prevent errors in credit reports!" This is not, however, the only things the act does.

It also prevents consumers from finding accountability for mistakes through limits on state influence in such credit disputes. Mierzwinski explains, "States can't regulate the industry to prevent errors in credit reports. States can't regulate the marketing of credit cards to consumers (the wordy little brochures we all get in the mail). States can't raise the low bar Congress set for consumer protections. States, in most cases, cannot give consumers the right to sue credit card companies that make costly mistakes –ultimately resulting in higher interest rates and higher premiums paid by a consumer for auto and home insurance, when furnishers report inaccurate information to the credit bureaus." This means that the only possible change must happen on the national level, forcing every consumer who has been wronged to literally "make a federal case out of it."

Sadly, industry lobbyists were able to get these permanent limits on state authority to enact stronger laws in areas of credit reporting during a major campaign in 2003. Not only the credit card companies, but every bank, every finance company, every mortgage company and every insurance company banned together to lobby for these limits, which prevent the states from enacting any consumer friendly law restricting the deceptive marketing of credit card offers to consumers. They also limit the authority of states to regulate credit card companies that make mistakes in reporting to the credit bureaus.

The industry claimed that this preemption was necessary because theirs is a national business—the rules have to be standard across the board. In other words, they attempted to argue that 50 states would come up with 50 different laws that the industry would have to deal with, causing legal turmoil. Mierzwinski objects, noting, "We all know it doesn't really work that way. The way it most often goes down is that a couple of states come up with ways to make things better for consumers and other states follow. Then, Congress finally enacts a law based on these couple of States pushing for good laws. Without [the states'] weight behind us, it is a much harder fought battle to see effective federal laws enacted."

When the lobbying worked and the industry got what it wanted, it was seen as a success for the entire financial industry. Consumer groups did get some of their longstanding demands met—but at a steep price. Sure, consumers can now get a free credit report and some identity theft protection. The industry's success in permanently limiting states' rights, however, drastically altered consumers' ability to turn to their states for protection. Mierzwinski says, "Congress is a very big ball to push up a hill, and it's much easier to get a push on it if we have the weight of good state ideas pushing as well. If you take away the right of the states to enact stronger laws, you almost guarantee that Congress will do nothing and will be captive to the regulated industries and their wealth of lobbyists. Congress rarely acts to protect consumers unless the states act first or there is a scandal—such as Enron."

The Fair and Accurate Credit Transaction Act of 2003 (FACTA), which added new sections to the federal Fair Credit Reporting Act (FCRA, 15 U.S.C. 1681 *et seq.*) is another example of intended pro-consumer legislation that has been manipulated in order to favor creditors instead. It was intended primarily to help consumers fight the growing crime of identity theft. Accuracy, privacy, limits on information sharing, and new consumer rights to disclosure are included in FACTA. (Pub. L. 108-159, 111 Stat. 1952). This was all good news for consumers, except that convoluted language contained in a little-known section of the act causes consumers to forfeit their FACTA rights if they use the assistance of a "credit repair organization" or CRO. The definition of CRO is so general in this passage that it could encompass licensed attorneys that assist consumers in exercising their FACTA rights. This paradox of law is typical of the loopholes found throughout, not only FACTA, but in consumer legislation in general, which makes navigating the process quite complicated for the average consumer.

I am not an attorney and don't pretend to be an all-knowing expert of these consumer protection laws. My story stems from real-life experiences that paint a picture of the lengths and affects an innocent consumer must face when a life has been turned upside down—through no fault of her own. Consumer protection laws created and intended to be a protective shield to aid us in finding necessary justice and accountability, have actually been spun into a wielding sword used against us. When the whole of my story has been told, the torturous and absurd length of it, I hope it will provide you with a much clearer view and understanding of why we must speak out to the need for reform in this system of greed and persecution, a system that has gone terribly wrong!

Some of the names have been changed to protect the innocent, or not so innocent.

Chapter 1 – My Identity—*Meet Me*

Have you ever woken up in the middle of the night trying to remember if you paid a bill? What if you woke up because you knew you did?

I was once an innocent, ordinary American with a near-perfect credit rating who made the unfortunate decision to make additional principal payments on my mortgage. As millions of ordinary Americans do on a regular basis, I wrote out a check every month and sent it in a timely manner, notating the additional monies being paid in the appropriate box as designated on the coupon payment booklet provided by my bank. This simple act of pre-paying my mortgage caused a grueling chain of events that left my once-ordinary life unrecognizable. This somewhat minor matter snowballed into a catastrophe that spanned a decade and forced me into two lawsuits. But –that's *not* what would initiate my passion to write this book. Not by a long shot. It would be the intrusive events that unfolded throughout the subsequent five years that would turn out to be the catalyst. To fully understand the story I'm about to unravel –you must first meet me.

As far back as I can remember I've been a woman filled with spirit and passion with a peculiar, yet undeniable, yearning to help others. That passion to help others was mystifying to me because I didn't know where it grew from or exactly how I was supposed to manifest it into action. I didn't know where or how to satisfy the urge inside me to make things better for someone—anyone. The same way some people claim they always knew, just knew, that they were going to someday become a doctor, lawyer, dancer, or actor, this drive to somehow benefit humanity was propelling me down my life path, leading me into the future.

I had often heard Oprah articulate the need to live an "authentic life" as well as the need to figure out what may be blocking us from living that life. Not living this authentic life has often been the source of that overwhelming feeling that *I know I am supposed to be doing something – but I don't know what the hell it is*. Oprah often urged her audience to find, and then face these cumbersome and often buried obstacles in our lives because they hold the key to peace and happiness. She held with certainty that once we figured out what was blocking us, all the uncertainty and confusion would dissipate. Clouds of confusion would give way to a bright, clear sky of clarity. I just could never, ever "get it," and trying to find the key or the blocks she spoke of was always a source of major frustration to me. Then it came— that *Aha* moment when suddenly pieces of my puzzled life began to fit together. Through divine guidance I began to view my life as though I was watching a slide show. It was obvious that one type of identity theft or another has been a leading theme in my life from the early age of thirteen. However, there would be none more prominent and none more damaging than the theft of my credit identity.

I was raised an Italian, Catholic girl. I attended summer catechism, grew up eating spaghetti three times a week and loved the overflow of family and friends my Nonie would gather every Sunday for her famous Italian dinners. I lived in a contemporary home with two sisters and a brother while being raised by my Mom and (a man I called) Dad. It wasn't until I turned thirteen that I found out that the man I had loved and called Dad for thirteen years, didn't technically merit the title. I came home from school one day and found an "adoption lady" sitting at the kitchen table. Without elaboration, they whisked me off to the courthouse a few miles away, where I became "adopted"—without fanfare or explanation–but legally, adopted. I later realized that the reason for my trip to the courthouse was the name I grew up with didn't match the name on my birth certificate and I was about to apply for a Social Security Card. In those days, you didn't file for a Social Security Card at birth as parents do now. It wasn't necessary to have a card, until you applied for a job. That momentous day was the first time I would feel my identity being ripped away from me–but it would be far from being the last time I would feel that way.

My parents were divorced my senior year of high school and much to my dismay, I felt my Dad "divorced" me as well. I was no longer felt viewed as his "real" daughter by him or my Mom, but rather a step-daughter. That, to their logic –released him from any responsibility for college tuition or support. With the swipe of a pen on their divorce papers it seemed my adoption, for all intents and purposes, was nullified–at least in my young eyes. I had grown to believe he was my *real* Dad and his title was deserved. Yet their actions made me feel as though my *identity* was stolen away again, without my having any say or control over it. As I grew older, I had developed an overwhelming desire to learn the identity of my biological dad—I suppose to help me find *me*. I questioned my Mom for years searching for his identity, but never leaned the truth. Finally, one Sunday afternoon, it seemed she apparently tired of my persistent and incessant prodding, and she abruptly divulged his identity. I learned he died when I was only eight but his legacy didn't. He was a well known, prominent business leader in our community. In one quick drop of my biological father's last name I immediately knew—I wasn't the full blooded Italian I grew up *believing* I was. There was no denying my identity had been changed again and with it came a new heritage—I suddenly learned I was half Jewish. I felt as though my true identity, the person I thought I was, continued to be altered by other people without my having any say or control. I began to wonder if I would *ever* have the power to rule my own identity, mold it and keep it safe from unwelcome changes. I never could have predicted that the hardest struggle to do so would involve an epic battle against corporate Goliaths—strangers, who for 15 years effectively stole my *true* identity.

Anyone who has ever suffered the effects of an identity theft will tell you first hand –it takes strength, stamina and often, years of your life to fix it. You suffer exhausting, agonizing frustration, just trying to regain your reputation and good name stolen from you. If creditors report false information to the credit bureaus as <u>factual</u> and they disseminate that information declaring its authenticity (even after you have proven your innocence), then the reflection of your credit history is not an accurate portrayal of you. It then becomes a personal assault on you, your family and your character, and changes *who* you are.

Identity theft is not just perpetrated by thieves using your social security number to obtain credit in your name. It is also perpetrated when corporate furnishers of information falsely portray you to be someone you are not. When a consumer works for years to build a good credit rating it can be stolen in a blink of an eye by corporations who continue to report (and sell) inaccurate data—without remorse, care or accountability.

I have learned more than I ever wanted to learn about the credit reporting industry and the justice system and hope that by my writing about my experience, failures, and hard-lessons learned it will cause you to pause and think about the changes you should make to better protect yourself. I have spent the last fifteen <u>consecutive</u> years writing dispute letters to refute fallacies in my credit file, fighting against mortgage servicing errors, and battling through two stressful lawsuits against powerful and manipulative opponents. I am not at all a litigious person. Nor am I irresponsible, whiny, or an isolated case. I was just very certain that I was not in the wrong, but nobody would listen. While my story may sound extreme, it's not at all a *unique* case, as the corporations involved purposely portray it to be. Let me assure you, problems such as mine are systemic. Those of us who have already suffered the effects of identity theft or inaccurate credit reporting can attest to an all-too-common characteristic—we can't get rid of it. This then, is the story that I will be unraveling for you in this book.

There is one basic fact that every consumer needs to be aware of–our consumer protection laws are eroding. This is largely due to the lobbying efforts of large corporations and the corrupting influence of those efforts (via campaign contributions) on our elected representatives. Crimes such as identity theft, corruption and fraud are exploding, and what happens daily to millions of innocent consumers <u>can</u> happen to you too. It doesn't matter if your bank account resembles that of Trump, Oprah, or the average working Joe –odds are, fraud will touch your life and alter it for years to come. This story will ring true to those of you who've unfortunately been living this nightmare, and hopefully, provide crucial knowledge to those of you that eventually will. Simply put, knowledge is power and consumers need all the power they can get in order to protect their assets –and good name. Without that all important knowledge, consumers are wide open to an array of problems that could find them as easily as they found me. It's not only opportunity, but also catastrophe, that can knock on your front door.

When my nightmare began, I was employed as a real estate paralegal, living in Western Massachusetts. It was a small, picturesque town called Greenfield, 20 or so miles across the border from Brattleboro, Vermont, where I was born and raised. I had been working in the real estate field since I moved to Massachusetts in my mid 20s. I began as a receptionist at the largest law firm in Franklin County: Levy, Winer, Hodos, Berson, Blanker and Bishop. It was Dick Bishop who hired me and it was also Dick that would become a valued friend and mentor. He took me under his wing and taught me the complexities of real estate transactions while I worked as their receptionist. He encouraged me to grow, giving me the skills to advance, and taught me to believe in myself. Through his mentoring, I did advance. I was initially promoted to Dick's personal secretary, and through his guidance, became his real estate paralegal.

I remember the day he came into my office with a smile on his face and hands behind his back as though he was hiding something. He pulled out a box of business cards that had my name and title of real estate paralegal beautifully engraved. He explained that along with those cards came my own assistant and another promotion. I was now also going to be responsible for handling his entire real estate load, both residential and commercial closings from start to finish and overseeing the sale of Title Insurance Policies to area attorneys. This move, he explained would allow him to focus his attention fully on his chosen field of estate planning while I managed his real estate practice. It was the real estate boom of the 80s and I would often find 13 or more closings in a week's time to be the norm. It was stressful, but I found it challenging and invigorating. I began to understand how a mortgage worked and learned that paying additional principal on a mortgage shaved off years of interest charges and could greatly reduce the term of the mortgage.

I continued to take on more responsibilities and began traveling to Boston for classes offered by MCLE (Massachusetts Continuing Legal Education). One particular day, I was on the train headed into Boston with Sally in tow. She was a new employee that I was training in real estate who was recently hired to work for a senior attorney, whose practice revolved heavily, almost solely, on real estate. Sally innocently referred to how pleased she was with her starting salary in light of the fact that she hadn't worked in real estate and needed training. Of course, what she didn't know was there was a rule within the firm that no one was to speak of their salary with any other employees, a rule that I was about to learn the purpose of and reasoning behind. I found that even though I had six years seniority and was "training" her in the real estate field, she was earning a much higher salary.

As fate would have it that particular day, I met up with Gary Gruber and Ellis Landset, two local real estate attorneys who founded the firm Gruber & Landset. Sally and I had lunch with Gary and Ellis, both of whom I had known from working on a variety of closings while representing our respective clients. Ellis told me that their longtime paralegal was taking her bar exam and would soon be leaving them.

"Denise, do you know of anyone that may be interested in a position with us?"

I paused, considering the salary information I just received from Sally. "Would any inquiries or resumes be confidential?" I asked.

"Yes," Ellis responded. "Just please have them contact me."

The next morning, the phone rang at my desk and Ellis was on the other end. I thought he was calling about a closing, but instead he asked, "Yesterday, when you asked me if any *response* would be confidential, by any chance were you contemplating any interest in this position for yourself?"

"Yes," I answered. "How did you know?"

"Just a feeling," he said. "Can you come over after work and meet with Gary and me and let us tell you about the position?"

"Sure," I said.

Why not? I thought to myself. I was going through an array of emotions traversing between hurt, anger, and disbelief after learning about the salary discrepancy and it wouldn't hurt to hear what they had to say.

I arrived at their office at 5:30. As they spoke, I couldn't help but notice how laid back the working atmosphere was in their offices. Both Gary and Ellis were children of the 1960s, very mellow and usually attired in denim around the office. They only dressed in suits for their appointments and then changed back to shorts or jeans, far different from the staunch, dress code atmosphere of a corporate firm. They made it clear they wanted me to come to work for them and were prepared to offer me whatever it was going to take to get me. It was flattering yet frightening at the same time.

It was an offer most would not refuse; a large salary increase, matching vacation time, regular bonuses, personal time and job flexibility. At Levy/Winer, we had the option to work ten-hour days, four days a week in the summer, even though the office was still open five days a week. In New England, the summers are short and many businesses opted for that additional day off to enjoy the nice weather. This new offer promised me a four day work week year round and total flexibility as to what day off I chose, as long as I arranged my day off around my work.

"Denise you'll run the show. When the work is there, you'll need to get it done. If you have a slow day or slow period, take the time off, leave early or come in late—whatever suits your work style. We know your work ethic and trust you will do whatever you have to do to get the job done. We'll accept any and whatever way works best for you."

Who would refuse that? As much as I respected Dick Bishop and fully appreciated and recognized how much he had done for me, it was an offer I had to consider. I told them I would need to think about it and if I did come to work for them, it would be necessary for me to stay with Dick until he found an acceptable replacement. The next day I went into Dick's office to tell him what happened on the train ride and during my meeting with Gary and Ellis. He immediately jumped up from his desk and ran upstairs. I found later he had called an emergency meeting with his partners. He was either as upset as I was that my salary didn't match or exceed an "untrained" new co-worker or distressed because it was his status as junior partner that affected the salary of his valued assistant—me. I would eventually find out, as I predicted, he had been fighting yearly to close the inequity of my salary but, in the world of corporate red tape, he had no power over the fact that salaries of senior partner employees were often measured by status, and not skill.

When Dick came back, he admitted he couldn't offer what Gary & Ellis had. He couldn't offer the casual dress, the ability to work four days a week year round, nor could he offer me the flexibility they could, due to obvious concerns of upsetting other employees. As much as he didn't want me to leave, he knew it was an offer I shouldn't refuse and as usual, continued to look out for me. Through tears, I gave him a month's notice and told him, if it took longer to find my replacement, not to worry, I would remain as long as it took.

As I looked up with teary eyes, he handed me an envelope.

"What's that?" I asked.

"It's a bonus check for your yearly review."

"That's not for two months! I can't take that, I just told you I'm leaving!"

"It isn't for next year Denise, it's for this last year. Your actions throughout the year prove you earned it and deserve it. It's your bonus."

I recognized him for his continuous generosity. Tears were streaming down my face as I remembered how much he had taught me over the years, questioning if my leaving was the right thing to do. Finally, he convinced me to seize the opportunity and to also take the rest of the day off recognizing how emotional this decision was for me to make. More importantly, he offered me his understanding and blessing.

I began working at Gruber & Landset and soon learned that Dick had stopped taking on real estate closings for a while, telling brokers, "Tragedy struck—Denise left." I felt horrible and still questioned if I was doing the right thing. Dick had told me I could always come back, which relieved my fear -just enough, that I was able to give the new position my best shot.

Gary and Ellis soon became like family to me. They were very easy to work for and the relaxed atmosphere was a blessing. No more fighting with my closet to make sure skirts were the right length, suits were picked up at the cleaners, my shoes weren't open-toed and no more fear that I wasn't dressed to the very high standards of the corporate law firm.

After working with Dick for six years and then Gary and Ellis for six years, I realized I had built a reputation in the legal community as a skilled paralegal who understood the field of real estate inside and out. I had developed the capability to fix the many problems that crop up in the course of a real estate transaction, often before anyone knew there was any trouble. Real estate has must-meet deadlines and closings fall apart at the last minute, creating a domino effect of more closings pushed into the following, already overloaded, week. A week with a tentative schedule of thirteen closings could easily turn into a week of twenty-three or more. Even when I felt that I was on top of everything, an avalanche of paperwork could fall. Juggling dates and times for closings can become the norm and changing schedules is not easy—sellers and buyers are under contract to sell or buy. They have movers lined up and contracts they must fulfill, making the only acceptable answer, "It must be done—period." The client could end up losing a good interest rate or be faced with an even bigger nightmare—one of the parties backing out of a contract, leaving the other party high and dry-and guess who can be held accountable? "Burn-out" claims many in the industry due to the never-ending—urgent deadlines, multi-tasking and time constraints that rule your world –everyday.

My entrepreneurial spirit began to kick into overdrive. Working for myself, I thought, could alleviate some of the stress. I thought that by providing additional time and flexibility, working at home would stop my personal "burn-out." I had 24 hours in a day and 7 days in a week to juggle at home rather than the mere 8 or 10 hours in an office. I could type many of the documents at night or even over the weekend, allowing me to take more time off during the week for my daughter's high school events. I would often find myself working in the office on weekends or bringing assignments home anyway. Therefore, doing all the work from home seemed to be a way to stop my growing stress. It would be an entrepreneurial move that would allow me to provide a unique service that had never been offered in the legal community before. I contemplated offering my services, on a sub-contracting basis, to area attorneys that needed assistance completing real estate closings.

Gary and Ellis didn't initially like the idea, feeling nervous that I would not be right there for them to turn to at any given moment. After I assured them that not only did I want to still do *all their* closings, I promised to always put their needs above those of others. They then reconsidered their stand and generously supported my move. After all, Gary and Ellis were not just my employers, they were my friends. We would often socialize outside the office and each of us knew every intricate detail of our children's lives, our health and our homes.

Establishing a home office was working out great for me. My client base included attorneys from two counties. Some of the lawyers practiced real estate and needed help taking a portion of the load off their overwhelmed staff of paralegals and secretaries. Others were attorneys that didn't practice in real estate but could now accept real estate clients by employing my services.

These attorneys would furnish me with the particulars of the borrower's or seller's name, property location and contact information. I would take over from there. I initiated the title, ordered all the necessary documents and inspections, completed the closings and delivered a completed and closed file. Soon I found myself busier than I had been working at the firm, having to turn away prospective new clients. Though it became one of the busiest times of my life, I couldn't have been happier.

I never could have imagined it was all going to come to an end. My real estate skills were top of the line and I knew the business inside and out. Perhaps naively, I believed that this expertise also aided me in the management of my own mortgage. I quickly found out that I was severely mistaken. A mere six months into starting my new and growing business, in January, 1992, I learned of accounting problems with my own mortgage when I innocently set out to refinance.

The mortgage was originally taken out in 1988. Over the years, we often paid additional principal on our mortgage while utilizing a payment coupon book provided by my lender. Each month I would rip out a coupon and clearly check the box where it indicated I was sending in additional money. I would place the exact breakdown of funds I was sending on the "balance on principal" line and also spelled out the amount of extra principal payment on the "memo" section of our check. For example, our payment was $577 and I would often send in a check for $600, notating the balance of $23 to be applied to principal. If I had additional funds from a tax return or savings, I would send it in the same way, checking the appropriate box on the coupon as well as marking both the check and coupon with the exact breakdown where indicated.

This is a common and recommended practice because these small additional payments can save a consumer thousands of dollars in interest and can significantly reduce the number of years necessary to pay off a mortgage. It allows future payments to be applied in your favor (more going to principal, less to interest) every month to follow. What I never realized at the time was that my careful notations on the coupon and my checks meant nothing if the bank didn't apply the money accurately. The payment coupon did not supply me with any proof of where my money actually went, which as it turns out, was often not where I had directed it to go. What exactly was my bank doing with my hard earned money? How were they handling my most important investment—my home? Without a breakdown and/or monthly statement to verify the accuracy of the application of my money, there was no way for me to know.

Before my own nightmare began, I never thought anything about it and I'm sure most of you don't either. Like I once did, you may be assuming and blindly trusting the largest asset of your life is safely accounted for correctly and carrying the correct balance. Banks have accounting systems and fail-safes that ensure payments are applied correctly... right? That presumption would be my first mistake and would cause a set of interlocking events I could never have imagined. I can guarantee that once you read this book, you will no longer make such presumptions.

I can't stress enough that without having access to a monthly statement that tracks and verifies how your payments are applied, you too could be in serious trouble and not know it.

Chapter Lesson: Your Credit Identity

Your name (and your identity) upon which you are known and increasingly judged is determined by your credit rating whether or not the data contained in your credit file is truthful or not. <u>Find your identity</u>! While the scores must be purchased separately, credit reports are free on an annual basis at **877-322-8228**. You can also receive a free copy if any of the following has occurred:

- You were denied credit, insurance or other services. In this case, you will receive a free copy only from the specific bureau whose report led to that denial.

- You were charged higher rates, fees or deposits. In this case as well, you will receive a free copy only from the specific bureau whose report led to those higher charges.

- You certify in writing that you are unemployed and plan to seek employment in the next 60 days

- You certify in writing that you are a welfare recipient

- You certify in writing that you have been a victim of fraud

Your credit files contain your:

- Personal data such as your birth date, aliases, current and previous addresses and employment

- Public records such as judgments, tax liens, notices of default and bankruptcies
- Credit data such as your account details, including payment history
- Inquiries (companies who reviewed your credit report) for the previous 12 to 24 months
- The credit bureaus (credit reporting agencies) only report what's reported to them by:
- Creditors and collection agencies who have accounts with the CRAs
- Data services supplying public record data
- You if you successfully dispute reported data

A mortgage held by a private party (seller, relative, etc.) cannot be added to your credit file because a private individual cannot report to the credit bureau. Only creditors have "subscriber contracts" with the bureaus allowing them to report data for a fee. According to the FCRA, they define what we commonly call a credit report as a "consumer disclosure" or "consumer report." Most of the time a creditor doesn't see the actual report. Rather, they are only provided with the three-digit credit score.

You should only purchase your credit report directly from the bureaus to avoid inquires by middle-men agencies being placed on your file. Remember: we don't have a choice when it comes to dealing with the "big three." There is no option as to whether you want them in your life or not, as you have when it comes to other corporations who vie for your business. The "big three" buy and sell your information without regard for its accuracy and the only control you have is to review your file closely and often. Take advantage of your free credit report and review your file. It is even more important to do so if you are about to refinance, purchase a home, buy insurance or an automobile because your interest rates are tied directly to your credit score. You will not get your score for free, but you can check your file for any discrepancies or possible errors and see what data is compiled in your report. You have to review <u>all three</u> of your credit reports and dispute inaccurate or incomplete data periodically if you want to ensure you are receiving the interest rate and/or low cost insurance you deserve. Again, your score is not automatically included in your credit report. You often have to pay extra money or jump through extra hoops to obtain that score. Plus, the score you are given is not necessarily the same score that is provided to creditors. Monitoring your credit report for errors is crucial to ensure you are not being judged on inaccurate information.

After all, consequences of a low credit score or an inaccurate credit report are not only financial. Once upon a time those facts were only used to determine our credit worthiness in repaying a loan or in an application for an extension of credit. Somehow, over the years, credit has developed into a tool used to judge our very identity—with far reaching effects. If you have a perfect driving record but have a low credit score, you will pay high risk premiums. If you apply for a job, or an apartment, that too can depend on that almighty credit report. The Transportation Security Agency (TSA) has even suggested using credit scores in the airline industry, much to the ACLU's displeasure. If that talk turns into a reality, people speculate that we may get our own newly-established colors. Certain people would be classified as "green—good to go," "yellow—extra security measures need to be taken," and "red," which may cause a denial of boarding. When and where does it end? Will our score be the determining factor of how many children we're allowed to have, what schools they can go to, what neighborhoods we are allowed to live in? What about how much we pay for groceries or clothes, or whether entrance to a particular restaurant will be allowed?

Increasingly, credit reports and scores are being utilized outside financial arenas in situations where there is no credit being extended. Insurance premiums that require up-front payment or job advancement are both examples of situations where your credit is evidence used to judge you. These situations have nothing to do with your capabilities but rather if you pay your bills on time or have debt of 30/60/90-day late payments. Errors contained in the accounting of your mortgage, student loans, and car payments can and do end up in your credit file and those errors can be costly. You just may learn those errors were the cause of a lost opportunity, denial of a loan or a job, or higher interest rates and insurance premiums.

Chapter 2 – *The Not-So Merry-Go-Round*

To fully understand the entire set of dominos that were about to crash down in my life, we must begin in January, 1992, the month and year that my unwanted ride on the not-so-merry-go-round was turned on. The ride would last nearly a decade before it was turned off, briefly –only to find it would be turned back on, for *at least* five more years –and counting.

One of my daily duties as a real estate paralegal was to order mortgage payoff statements for my clients when a homeowner was selling or refinancing a home. In order to refinance or sell, a homeowner must know the exact amount of money the bank requires before discharging the current mortgage on the home. On this unsuspecting, particularly cold and snowy New England day back in 1992, I contacted my bank regarding my own mortgage to do just that—find out what my payoff would be so I could refinance. I had calculated the approximate dollar amount that should be needed to payoff the mortgage. When I called to obtain the payoff amount, I quickly learned my estimate and the amount the bank calculated appeared to differ by several thousand dollars—not a trivial difference.

"Don't worry," the representative from my local Shawmut Bank in Amherst, assured casually. "While your balance isn't what you thought it should be, you are paid up until November." So ominous were these words that I felt them echoing through that phone line: *Don't worry, worry, worry...*

I jumped up out of my seat and right before I landed on the floor I heard the words streaming out of my mouth, "I'm paid up until November? The *November* that is 11 months from now?"

"Yes, nearly a year in advance," he nonchalantly answered.

It may have taken me a moment but I quickly understood there was trouble. I realized that throughout the life of my mortgage beginning in 1988, I never received a monthly statement that provided me with a breakdown as to how my payments were (or were not) applied. By paying my mortgage with the provided coupon book, I wasn't able to verify how <u>any</u> of my payments were applied, but quite honestly never felt there was a need to worry. However, I knew that if I was paid in advance they must have taken our extra principal payments and broken them down into monthly pre-payments, making it appear that our account was "paid in advance." I quickly asked for a payment history break down (known as an amortization schedule or payment history schedule) to be mailed to me. When I finally received it in the mail and reviewed their accounting of my payments detailing how my money was being applied, the magnitude of their errors began to emerge.

As I looked over the entire history, I became very concerned. The payment history schedule they provided me reflected many of my payments had been wholly applied to interest. Often I found that on some months not a single cent was applied to the principal balance. On other occasions, it reflected that I was penalized with bogus late fees for payments made on time or actually paid early. Thankfully, I had saved all my cancelled checks. With the knowledge that I was never late on my payments, I set out to trace all my payments back to the beginning of the loan to prove to them that their accounting was seriously flawed.

As an example, I had paid my February 1st payment on January 23rd. However, I found they had erroneously applied that payment as a *late January payment* and then penalized me with an erroneous $25.00 late fee! That meant that my additional $23+ I had included in my check marked for "additional principal payment" was unknowingly eaten up in inaccurately processed late fees along with *daily* illegal interest charges that accrued as well. I additionally found that a $3,000 principal payment made a year earlier was applied as "payments in advance" and not to the principal balance of the loan as directed. All of this was unknown to me because I never had the ability to verify how my payments were applied. I, like countless others, blindly trusted the bank and their accounting methods while paying my mortgage with their provided payment coupon book. How could I verify how my payments were being applied— or in my case, and I would bet many others—misapplied?

Additionally, under the law, consumers have a 15-day grace period before any penalty can be assessed. However, in reviewing the Shawmut payment history schedule and my cancelled checks, I found another disturbing trend. The cancelled check was stamped with the date received, yet the dates of their deposit and their credit to my account, were often times many days apart. I'd then be penalized and charged for additional interest for each day my payment wasn't applied to my account.

From the moment I found out about the many mistakes contained in my mortgage, I was very proactive in contacting Shawmut. I made countless calls and seemed to speak to countless bank representatives, each with their own promises that their "research" would resolve the matter. It soon became crystal clear that no matter how many phone calls I made, Shawmut didn't know how to correct their errors and calculate the true balance owed. These mistakes were so monstrous that they would begin to take on a life of their own as each initial bank error began to compound monthly. It compounded and compounded until the true balance of the loan was impossible to figure out. Each misapplication of my payments meant costly increased interest payments. If they had applied the funds accurately on the dates they received the payments, every payment made thereafter would benefit me, with more of my money going toward the principal and less applied to interest.

I grew fearful that Shawmut didn't have the proper accounting skills or procedures necessary to correct their errors –or they just didn't want to. This was obvious a short time later when I was actually told, *"Look, you say your balance is one thing and we think it's another. Why don't we pick a number in the middle and call us even?"*

I was shocked. Can you imagine a consumer asking that of a bank? Can you imagine a consumer saying, "Look, you say I owe $25 in late fees and I think I owe you nothing? Let's pick a number in the middle and we'll call us even?" We all know the answer to that question yet somehow, through my bank's arrogance, they thought it was an acceptable answer to the problems they were *solely* responsible for. What was worse, I failed in getting anyone to actually hear me and therefore take effective measures to address my concerns. It was very frightening that there seemed to be no end in sight, leaving me paying higher interest rates and unable to refinance.

Many representatives promised they would "fix" the problems by sending it off to research. Just like the ominous suggestion not to worry, these words echoed from the telephone many times—*sending it to research, to research, research...* I tried to convey to every representative how many times I'd already heard that exact speech. I could have recited it word for word. Knowing that it probably wouldn't do any good, I told them to send me their findings as soon as they finished their investigation.

Because they insisted I was paid in advance, I was told to "hold off sending in any more payments while the file is in the research department." I didn't feel safe doing that nor did I understand how not sending in payments would help to correct their errors. I informed Shawmut of that fear and they responded, "Send in only *principal payments*, then. Whatever money you send will go directly towards the balance. All of it will be cleared up when we figure out how to correct the account and credit you with the interest deserved." As they instructed, I sent in a check for the normal amount of $600 the next month yet I marked the whole amount as "principal only." The next month came and my bank now indicated I was paid over a year in advance! The same errors that Shawmut had been making all along without my knowledge, were now continuing as I watched it. It wasn't getting better as promised—it was only getting more complicated. More and more days went by and more and more phone calls were made as time began slipping away. Each payment history schedule they sent would have to be sent back with notations of corrections and, regardless, the next "updated" schedule they sent me was never up to date and never accurate.

It was obvious that I had no way to determine how they were applying my checks at this point and relayed my concerns to yet another Shawmut representative. Yet another faceless bank representative assured me that the best solution would be to stop sending in <u>anything</u> until the whole account was cleared up. It seemed a better option than continuing with the obviously detrimental "principal only" payments they had urged me to send in. Many different customer service representatives had all confirmed that our account was prepaid for well over a year and agreed that it would be best not to send anything in at all until they could clear it up. I begrudgingly followed that guidance (for two months) and it turned out to be the worst advice yet.

On a normal, quiet Saturday morning, less than a month after their advice not to send in payments during their investigation, I received the phone call that initially dropped me to my knees. "This is Sharon Caughman from Shawmut Bank. I'm calling to inform you that Shawmut is calling in your loan."

"What?" I demanded, asking her where on earth she was getting this information. Sharon said that a file landed on her desk showing we were three months behind on our mortgage. My heart was in my throat and I had no idea how to articulate what we had been through. This quaver in my voice was a product of a whole year of frustration at this point, and with fear seeping into my veins, I tried to explain. "I have documentation to prove we're not behind. Furthermore, three short weeks ago we were paid over a year and a half in advance. "I've been trying to get Shawmut to fix their errors for a year! I have saved every single check!"

She seemed sympathetic and advised; "If you could make even one payment today and send it out in overnight mail, I can keep the file in my hands . . ." Remember that, she said <u>her</u> hands. She continued, ". . . long enough to do something about it." She was apologetic about my struggle and seemed genuinely empathetic to my situation. If what I said was true, she said, and we were not delinquent on our payments, Shawmut had no legal means to call in our loan or begin foreclosure proceedings. I felt relieved to finally have an understanding ear on the other end of the Shawmut line, especially one with a name and capable hands she was keeping our file in. Sharon instructed me to get my payment into her and then give her seven days to see what she could do. She gave me her extension and advised me that within a week she would get back to me.

No matter how much I wanted to believe in Sharon however, I had dealt with too many of Shawmut's representatives to fully put my trust in this one woman. I sent in the payment as Sharon directed but, as the hours after the call passed, I grew angry at Shawmut's disregard for my personal struggle. The audacity of them to call us this way, threatening to call in the loan after all the trouble they had put us through with their now compounded errors. After a week went by with no call from Sharon, I called her. When I dialed her extension, someone else picked up. I asked to speak with Sharon but to my horror I heard the words, "Sharon? She no longer works in this department."

I think I was in shock for a moment, remembering her promise that by my sending in "just one payment" she could keep it "in her hands." *Now whose hands was this mess of a mortgage in?* I requested to be transferred to whichever department she now worked in. The woman on the other end, Lynn St. Marie, put me on hold. She was gone a few minutes. When she came back on the line, she apologized and informed me, "Nobody knows where Sharon went." *Nobody knows where Sharon went . . . in her hands, her hands . . .* Was I a victim of some type of cruel joke that everyone knew about but me?

There simply were no words to adequately express how I felt. It was beyond comprehension how this could continue, but I would be about to discover that this was nothing—nothing at all. The carnival ride had only just begun. Now I had another Shawmut voice on the line wanting to know what my problem was. I felt that I could have tape recorded my story months ago and just kept pressing play. Then again, all of these rotating bank representatives may just as well have been tape recordings themselves. They would pause long enough for me to cry, explain, and have my frustrated tirade, and then the rotating recorded messages would kick in again: *"I'll have to send your file to research,"* they would say. *"You should receive something in the mail in a few days,"* they soothed. Then there was the ever-constant reassurance, *"Don't worry."*

As I was speaking to this new Shawmut representative, Lynn, I suddenly felt a wave of fear come over me. *Am I going to lose my home?* Out of complete and utter frustration, I began crying inconsolable tears.

"I'll have to send this off to be researched but you should get their findings in just a few days," she said.

Much to my surprise, a letter from Shawmut did arrive in the mail just a few days after that conversation. Unfortunately, instead of the research department findings, it was a notice informing us that our loan was three months past due. I called Lynn immediately. She told me that though she hadn't heard anything back from research, I needed to send in three months worth of payments straight away. She emphasized that the only way to ensure that the bank didn't call in our loan was by making these payments.

Where were we going to pull together an additional $1733? Why was it necessary? We had to do some financial magic and round up $1733 or we could lose our home, I thought. I feared that failure in this instance might lead us into a foreclosure. My heart continued to pound and I was literally sick to my stomach, doubled over in the bathroom. When I could extricate myself from the house, I went to the post office to mail our check, via certified mail and to the attention of Lynn, to the new address in Connecticut she provided.

A few days passed and Lynn called me with what seemed to be excellent news. She had received my three payments, thankfully, and was happy to inform me that the bank had finally fixed their errors. There were no more problems with my account. This information initially relieved me because Shawmut was finally acting to fix the problems that they created, or so I thought. Then I heard...,

"We applied the lump sum of all those pre-payments to your account on February 9, 1993."

"WHAT?!" Once I caught my breath, I realized my relief was short-lived. It still wasn't right. I hadn't made the lump sum payments in February 1993! My payments were scattered throughout the many prior years. By crediting payments in a lump sum as of an arbitrary date in 1993, it meant that all the payments I made prior to that date didn't benefit from reduced interest charges. I didn't receive the interest credit that I should have earned, making their proposed solution very costly to me. Would they let me pay them a year late without incurring late fees? Never. While I lost out, it was a great move for Shawmut. They had an interest free loan on my money for a year!

I explained all of this to Lynn and insisted this was still unacceptable. I then heard a familiar echo in reply—*I will send it to research, to research, research . . .*

Lynn was out to lunch when I called the next time and I was finally able to speak with Alan, the illusive supervisor that I had left many messages for but never had the privilege to speak with. Alan introduced himself as the Head of Collections. He listened patiently as I rattled through my story. He too apologized for the mess the bank had put me through and said he would "personally make sure someone from Consumer Relations got in touch."

"No, no," he replied to my questions. "Your account will not be reported to the credit bureaus."

He then apologized for the bank's errors and told me that he couldn't believe how poorly my account had been handled. I wish I would have recorded him when he agreed with me by saying, "If Shawmut had done the right thing the first time you called, an entire year of problems would have been avoided."

As usual, I didn't hear from Shawmut Consumer Relations. I eventually received a copy of an "internal memo" Lynn St. Marie had sent to another Shawmut representative requesting further research on my account. Included with the memo was a payment history schedule. What I reviewed on this latest payment history report can only be described as an outright maze of negligence and deceit. The history was littered with "interest charges" marked "computer generated." These appeared to be charges accrued when, at their insistence, I didn't make two payments while they continued to "research" their errors and correct misapplied "pre-payments." Interest and principal payments were all mixed up. The original $3,000 lump payment was still recorded a year late. Remember my February payment, the $1773 that Shawmut demanded in order to prevent my defaulting on the loan? Well...that money went <u>entirely</u> to interest. Many of my payments were being eaten up in interest charges because, while I was paid in advance and they told me to stop activity, they neglected to tell me that once they had it straightened out—put my payments where they were suppose to be—they were going to charge interest from the time the last payment was made to the time they got it fixed.

I called Alan and went through the numbers that were hand-written and scratched all over the paper. He told me he was the person responsible for these latest finding and wanted to know specifically which *numbers* I had issue with. As I recited the laundry list of costly mistakes, I saw clearly that every piece of advice, every word of instruction, had the effect of putting more money in their pocket at my expense. As I put all the errors together, piece by piece from this document, I was amazed that this confusing and continuously wrong statement was the purported proof they were forwarding to me to show me that everything was "fixed." When Alan and I were finished, more *research* needed to be done. Of course.

After this round of investigation, Lynn sent me a letter informing me that she was able to verify that a few of my payments had been corrected. They were credited to the proper day and interest charges were recalculated from the payment date. She didn't include a new payment history as proof or any other documentation for me to verify this—just her word. At this point, I was not in the mood to believe in anything without proof.

None of the various payment history schedules to date had been even close to being correct. I called the bank and ended up back on the phone with Alan. "This accounting is still completely unacceptable and I'm not going to rest until the fees and inappropriate interest charges had been corrected. He was of no help. I had lost track of the number of times I had attempted to correct my problems internally with Shawmut. This was the point where I finally threw up my hands and turned to others for help.

I contacted The Massachusetts State Consumer Fraud Protection Office. I had saved every paper I received from Shawmut. I copied every letter and wrote down everything I could remember from each conversation, including names and dates. Paper became my life. During that period, my very existence centered on the creation and storage of paper, the latter act being more important than I ever knew. I would become thankful for that hoarding and even sharing my experience now, my journals have proved invaluable in providing details. Every financial ordeal has a heart of paper. Documents, money, letters, cancelled checks—everyone wanted paper from me to prove my credibility and to prove my innocence. I found it ironic that my bank provided me with payment coupon books instead of a monthly statement in a move they purported was a more cost effective, less cumbersome, paper-saving method. Yet, when an error occurs, they would accept nothing less than every paper ever created to prove your innocence. In this arena, you are guilty until you prove yourself innocent, repeatedly.

Contacting the Consumer Fraud Protection Office was the first step on the way to the courthouse. I am not a litigious person and perhaps that is why, prior to my initiating a suit against Shawmut, I spent two exhaustive years trying to make the bank fix their own mistakes by myself. I didn't go running to the courts joyfully. Rather, I went kicking and screaming with the knowledge of the strength it would take to go through those intimidating, costly courtroom doors. However, I firmly believed that I had done no wrong. I thought that my situation was like purchasing a car which breaks down month after month. I did everything the dealer instructed me to do yet find that nothing seems to fix the problem. In that case, I would think that I had bought a "lemon," and would have the ability to assert my rights to another car under what's known as the "Lemon Law." I saw my situation just as straightforwardly— Shawmut had sold me a lemon.

Chapter Lesson: The Anatomy of a Mortgage

Many people have asked how paying additional "principal only" payments aids in both reducing the amount of interest payable and effectively reduce the term of the loan. Whether it's a student loan, car payment or mortgage payment, as long as there isn't a pre-payment penalty contained in the loan contract or mortgage it can save thousands of dollars in interest and shave years off the life of the loan. Again, I cannot advise doing so without verifying how the money is applied each time that additional payment is sent in.

A conventional fixed rate mortgage payment includes both the interest, and the reimbursement of principal to the lender. With each monthly payment being divided between interest and principal, any additional principal payments are applied directly to the principal balance of the loan. That translates into a smaller balance due on the outstanding balance of the loan, from which interest is calculated and, therefore, reduces the monthly interest due each time you lower your outstanding balance with an additional payment.

The monthly payment remains the same, but the amount of principal is reduced. If a consumer wants to pay off his loan faster and save on interest, this method is great. If he is looking to lower the monthly payment due, this method will not work. Here is an example:

Sample	30 year fixed rate-**regular monthly** payment	**One lump** additional Principal Payment	**Monthly additional** payments
Loan amount:	$ 150,000	$ 150,000	$150,000
Loan term (months):	360	360	360
Interest rate:	6.25%	6.25%	6.25%
Mortgage payment:	$ 923.58	$923.58	$923.58
Additional principal payment:	$0	$1,000.00	$20.00
Total payments:	**$ 332,487**	**$327,130**	**$319,696**
Interest expense:	$ 182,487	$177,130	$169,696
Life of loan (months):	360	354	339
Life of loan (years):	30	29.5	28.25

The table shows a comparison between a 30-year fixed-rate mortgage with no additional principal payments, a mortgage with one lump-sum additional principal payment and a mortgage where a small amount is added to each monthly mortgage payment. You can realize a sizable savings when making a lump sum payment or simply making one additional payment a year. By their "pre-paying" my mortgage and failing to apply additional funds towards the principal, my savings diminish and theirs profits rise. There are many mortgage company and consumer web sites (such as bankrate.com and cardratings.com) that have free calculators for consumers to utilize. By plugging in personal information, consumers can find the best solution for their needs. Many consumers are surprised to learn how much time they can shave off their loan and are shocked to see how much interest they can save simply paying a little extra.

Shawmut labeled my account "paid in advance" as opposed to applying my additional payments on the principal, leaving the true balance of my mortgage nearly impossible to determine because it went undiscovered for too long. Without having the aid of a monthly statement, I had no way of knowing my payments weren't applied as intended and indicated on my coupons. Had they wanted to correct it, they could have if they sat down and recalculated my payments –by hand, something they refused to do. By applying payments as "paid in advance" payments, instead of directly applying to the principal, it is essentially like placing money in a drawer or in a jar buried in the backyard—it affords no benefit to the consumer. That buried money, however, is given to the bank to do with what they please, free, for the year or two their customer is paid in advance. Essentially, the bank gets an interest-free loan on the consumer's money.

Errors in Adjustable Rate Mortgages (ARMs) are very common. In fact, the Federal Savings and Loan Insurance Corporation estimated in 1995 that consumers overpaid on their ARMs by more than $8 million due to bank errors in the computation of interest rates. Their study also showed that between 50 and 60 percent of all ARMs contain at least one error due to interest rate miscalculation. These apparently small errors can add up to big losses for a consumer. For instance, according to Real Estate Weekly's calculations, an interest rate that is off by only 0.462 percent could cause an extra $250 of overcharges a month on a $650,000 loan with a 10 percent interest rate. In 3 years, that little difference could cost a homeowner over $10,000!

Chapter 3 – *A little help from my friends*

      I collected all my paperwork, cancelled checks and correspondence with Shawmut and presented it to the Massachusetts Northwest District Attorney's Office where I filed a formal complaint against Shawmut. I also wrote a letter of complaint to my State Attorney General's Office and the State Banking Commission. Upon reviewing my documentation, the District Attorney's Office, Consumer Division, began their involvement by sending Shawmut a letter. They indicated that Shawmut "needed to sit down with the Richardsons and manually go through all the cancelled checks they supplied and re-calculate the mortgage." Furthermore, they asked Shawmut to address my concerns in person as opposed to continuing by way of phone calls and letters because that had proved entirely ineffective.

      Shawmut's reply was consistent with their previous actions, yet this time displayed greater arrogance. In one small move, they summarized their incompetence by mailing me yet another incorrect amortization schedule and a letter reciting Connecticut State Law. This letter claimed that Shawmut had legally and dutifully fulfilled their obligations, and in fact, I owed them money. The letter ended by insisting that I choose between the two enclosed options...the inaccurate amortization schedule calculations of the past, or the newly enclosed calculations that claimed I owed even more money due to alleged accrued interest charges.

      I looked through both documents carefully with my cancelled checks and found each accounting riddled with costly errors. I contacted Shawmut and explained that neither option was realistic. Their response stunned me. They insisted their offer to give me a choice was a "courtesy." Further, through their investigations, they had determined that the handling of my account had been "proper." I continued to contact Shawmut and they continued to ignore me.

Since a governmental letter requesting a formal meeting was not enough to push them to act, I decided I needed to make full use of *any* available government resources. I wrote both my legislators and the Federal Trade Commission but it was the Consumer Protection Office in Greenfield that finally became my new ally. Again, they officially, as a government entity, asked Shawmut to sit down and discuss my loan "*in person.*" Even then, efforts to get Shawmut to review the account with me went ignored. The bank refused these requests in writing by claiming that their headquarters were in a "*secured area consumers are not allowed in.*" The Consumer Protection Office conveyed to me "We've never seen anything like this." They seemed very empathetic to my situation. They, too, had lost faith that anyone at Shawmut could correctly get to the bottom of what I actually owed. I was determined to persevere and we eventually compelled Shawmut to agree to a meeting in their Greenfield branch.

I gathered my arsenal of documents and drove to the meeting. When the Shawmut representative, Mr. Rainer, pulled up my loan on the computer, his face seemed to flush and his eyes grew wide as if he couldn't believe what he was viewing on the screen. I was numb and at this point, I wouldn't have been shocked—if he pulled up my account and now found my debt to be tripled! I wouldn't have batted an eye. This Shawmut representative, however, relayed that not only was I entirely right about my account reflecting many serious inaccuracies, but it was clear that Shawmut had some serious internal accounting problems, as well as some possible *legal* ones, if this were to continue. As he seemed an empathetic and capable man, I volunteered to meet in person as many times as the bank needed to help resolve these problems. Mr. Rainer took copies of all the documentation I brought with me. I asked if he felt this could be resolved before the end of the year. It was already December 1993, just a month shy of two years since that fateful day in

January 1992, when I called Shawmut seeking an accurate mortgage payoff figure! I didn't want to begin another year like this. "Your account," he said, "is my number one priority and you have no need to worry." *Don't worry, worry, worry . . .* He then continued to say that he would submit my complaint, with the provided documents and with his findings. I should hear back from him or someone with authority at Shawmut shortly. There were those catchphrases again—bright yellow warning signs of more pain to come.

As the meeting drew to a close, I relayed to Mr. Rainer that while I hoped that these issues would be resolved by the bank, if they were not, I was ready to take the next step. I reminded him that my next step would have to be the justice system and the filing of what is known in Massachusetts as a Chapter 93A letter, a Massachusetts law established as a mini-Consumer Protection Act. The statute allows for individuals to receive double or treble damages in addition to any appropriate legal fees if a consumer's allegations of negligence and the validity of their claim are proved. The business on the receiving end of a Chapter 93A Letter has 30 days to resolve the problems addressed or dispute the claim before further legal action can be taken. Mr. Rainer assured me that my concerns would be taken care of. He told me again not to worry and we parted.

I <u>did</u> worry –but silently hoped he could fix the problems once and for all, now that I had been allowed to meet with him face to face. Since he promised correcting my mortgage balance would be a top priority, I silently prayed that a miracle would happen and he had the power to facilitate a resolution without the necessity of a law suit.

I received my first communication from Shawmut a few weeks after my face-to-face meeting with Mr. Rainer. As with most of this, my personal reality show, I realized in retrospect that I should have known what was coming. Maybe I was too idealistic, naive or optimistic. Shawmut's written "analysis" of my meeting that came in the mail wasn't the expected correspondence from Mr. Rainer but rather a short, arrogant letter from yet another Shawmut representative. The note stated, in no uncertain terms, that I was clearly mistaken to think that my account had been in any way mishandled. To prove their point they even included the prior payment history schedule, the same one that had glaring errors, from April 1993.

Shawmut didn't even bother to update or amend a nine month old payment history schedule, which proved to me that my meeting with Mr. Rainer had done no good. I phoned Mr. Rainer to ask if this letter was Shawmut's "official" response to our meeting and he explained that he received a copy of the same letter. He was astonished himself and had no explanation or excuse for their response. Promises to fix their errors were again broken. I believed they were being malicious and unremorseful about the suffering their actions caused me financially, physically and emotionally. I realized in hindsight I was the fool for letting them string me along as they did and decided to throw myself full-force into the justice system.

"I think I am going to have to go the route of a Chapter 93A letter," I told him. "It seems to be my only option."

Mr. Rainer paused and said, "Perhaps that is the only way you will get their attention."

I thought of another way to get their attention...go public! I wrote a Letter to the Editor of our local paper the Greenfield Recorder.

An Open Letter to Shawmut Bank

In 1988, we signed a fixed rate equity loan with Shawmut Bank. When numerous bookkeeping errors were discovered over 2½ years ago, we immediately brought them to your attention. Continual endurance on our part and what we believe to be knowing and willful disregard on your part has caused us to realize our only assurance of resolving these issues is through a court of law. After countless broken promises by more than 14

Shawmut Bank representatives in Worchester, Hartford, Boston and Greenfield, to resolve these ongoing problems produced by Shawmut Bank, the errors have grown to a magnitude where the correct balance of our account is unattainable.

Continual errors have been made while applying our monthly payments and our "extra principal" payments made to Shawmut Bank. When additional principal payments were made, they were not applied as principal reduction, but rather, applied as "payment in advance" never applying an interest credit. To correct your errors, your instructions were to "Pay principal payments only" while our account was being "researched." This generated additional interest which proved to be further damaging to our account.

Furthermore, both FDIC and the Consumer Protections Office have on at least three occasions requested that you sit down with us and by hand recalculate our loan. Shawmut refused, saying their corporate headquarters in Hartford were

"in a secured area where consumers were not allowed in." In December of 1993, after my repeated insistence, I was finally allowed to meet with a Shawmut representative in Greenfield, who reviewed the documentation and canceled checks that I provided. The representative acknowledged Shawmut did in fact have bookkeeping problems and stated that our account would now become a "top priority." Since that meeting more than nine months ago Shawmut has failed to take any effective measures in correcting out account or preventing further damage.

Your conscious disregard for our rights as consumers has prompted us to engage in raising public awareness of Shawmut's accounting practices which are undisclosed to consumers. This includes Shawmut's practice, which is contrary to local banks, that it does not honor a 15-day grace period without accruing additional interest and Shawmut's practice of not applying payments on the date of receipt but rather the day after receipt of payment, even if paid in the morning hours of the prior day. These influential facts must be disclosed to consumers to permit them to make a knowledgeable decision when obtaining a loan.

We strongly encourage consumers to call 1-800-SHAWMUT and request a "payment history schedule" enabling them to verify how their monthly payments are being applied. We also advocate banking with local community banks where consumers feel important and respected, not ignored and neglected.

The public response to my letter was phenomenal, yet unpredicted and terrifying. Even though I lived in Greenfield, a small town of approximately 22,000 people, Shawmut was a large New England Bank. Word spread like fire from Greenfield to Boston and neighboring New England States. Phone calls were pouring in from other Shawmut customers as well as customers from other "big" national banks who had similar problems. I was both stunned and alarmed when I found out that I was not alone, not by a long shot.

After going public with my story, it didn't take long for me to see that something was very wrong not only with my situation but within the banking industry as well. I learned that some consumers had lost their homes, and others were living in fear that they were about to, due to mishandled mortgages at the hands of giant, impersonal banks like Shawmut. It didn't take long to determine the obvious common denominator—payment coupon books. So many consumers were forced to blindly trust that our banks were applying our payments accurately. Without monthly statements, we had no way of verifying how our payments were applied, no knowledge of what fees we may have been charged, or any proof that extra principal payments or escrow monies for taxes and insurance were accounted for. Electric companies, cable companies and credit card companies supply us with monthly statements which provide us with proof that they accurately applied our previous month's payment. It is only common sense to the average consumer, to provide us with such statements. Why weren't the banks mandated to do so with our homes, our largest investment? I continued to find consumers who would confess, "We thought there were safeguards in place to account for our money. We trusted them."

I contacted my State Senator, Stanley Rosenberg. After relaying my personal nightmare, I asked if he would sponsor a proposed Bill mandating banks to provide consumers with monthly mortgage statements—basically outlawing payment coupon books in the mortgage industry. I circulated petitions to ban coupon payment books in various neighborhood stores, hoping to gather 100 or so signatures over the weekend. Astonishingly, with very little effort, in one weekend alone I received over 700 signatures. Senator Rosenberg and his staff soon became my strongest allies.

This proposed change in banking practice was not only considered necessary by the consumers who signed my petition, but it seemed a necessary measure to Senator Rosenberg as well. After forwarding my collection of signatures to Senator Rosenberg's office, with the promise of many more to follow, it grew easy to see that he "got it" and would became a passionate ally in my quest for consumers to have access to monthly statements. He shared his (now prophetic) fears that the small community banks would someday be replaced by these mega-banks and felt strongly that there should be accountability to consumers by affording them the necessary tools to track how their payments were being applied. He offered to sponsor the Bill and soon the local media began to take interest—an interest that Shawmut clearly didn't like.

Chapter Lesson: The Power of Paper

Keeping track of a mortgage can be a difficult undertaking, especially when lenders don't supply their customers with monthly statements, providing the necessary tool to verify how payments are actually applied. The ball is often in the consumer's court in terms of record-keeping and checking for accuracy. Through my own experience, I can recommend several important steps that will aid any homeowner both in ensuring their mortgage is being adequately handled and preparing for dispute if mistakes are found.

- **Keeping Copious Records:** Every piece of paper a consumer receives with regard to a complaint or loan payment should be kept and filed away for safekeeping. These types of receipts and records, a dispute generates, can help if you ever find you have to prove your innocence. Document, document and document- every person you have spoken to and on what date. Log it in a journal, date book or calendar and file all your receipts in a file for any future need -nothing supports a charge of faulty record-keeping *against* a lender more than the meticulous records of a consumer.

- **Using the Phone:** So many interactions occur by telephone, which makes documentation difficult. When using the phone, be sure to keep track of conversations in a phone log or journal. When speaking with a representative, ask for their first and last name, what department, and his/her supervisor's name. They often work in teams, so ask for their team number. Call centers tend to have high turnover rates and, therefore, when a representative leaves the company, a consumer will still have a superior to speak with about the case. A personal journal or date book and even a calendar, can often be deemed admissible in a court of law if a consumer can prove the records were written as the phone calls occurred and not, for example, days or weeks later. This proves that the records are reliable and cannot be called hearsay (basically, rumor) in a court of law.

- **Using the Mail:** Always, always use certified mail. Never address a letter "To Whom it May Concern." Always write to a real human being and, if you don't get results, work up the chain of command all the way up to the board of directors. If you don't get a response, send copies out again marked "second request".

- **Confirm it:** A consumer should always ask, by phone or mail, *"Will you send me something to confirm that?"* If possible, that confirmation should be a copy of the UDF, (universal data form), which creditors use to communicate with credit bureaus and collectors. You should even take this one step further by asking that a UDF be sent to all of the consumer's creditors. Credit card companies can raise rates and lower available credit limits without notice if negative information, (even if it is false) comes to their attention.

Chapter 4 – *Meeting Goliath*

Even though my path was leading in the direction of the courthouse, my additional efforts to draw attention to the systemic problem of coupon books continued to gain momentum with Senator Rosenberg's support. I grew to admire and respect Senator Rosenberg and only wish we had more politicians like him. He stayed in touch to let me know when the Bill we were sponsoring was scheduled to come up for discussion and asked that I speak personally on the merits of this proposed Bill. "I will be there." I assured him.

In the meantime, I had to find an attorney willing to go up against Shawmut. This was no simple task. Shawmut was a large bank that conducted voluminous real estate closings. In order for an attorney to represent borrowers and/or Shawmut, that attorney had to be listed as a "Shawmut Qualified Attorney." If an attorney practicing real estate stepped up to take on Shawmut, his real estate practice could be severely affected. He would most likely be banned from the bank's approved attorney list, which would kill his real estate practice. With the prospect of being black-balled from Shawmut's all-important list, it wasn't going to be easy to find an attorney that would risk losing huge bread and butter referrals, effectively biting the hand that feeds him.

Eventually, I found an attorney that understood the basics of a real estate mortgage and wasn't on Shawmut's "Qualified Attorney" list. Betty agreed to meet with me and examine all of my documentation but the process would have to be conducted on an hourly fee basis. At this point, I felt I had no other choice than to accept this lawyer's terms because I still was unable to refinance. Nor could I seem to get Shawmut to rectify their now compounded errors all by myself. After meeting with Betty, she agreed to take them on and I felt a huge sense of relief. She felt that now that my problems with Shawmut had become public, through my Letter to the Editor, their desire would be to shut me up. If they had this attitude, they would be less arrogant and more amicable about finding a resolution.

Hours of working on the case turned into days and days translated into money. Betty was taking this case on an hourly basis and I was being billed at $100 per hour, paid weekly. We began with reviewing the various pieces of paper from Shawmut; my checkbook and cancelled checks, my mortgage and note, all my notes from the Massachusetts Consumer Protection Bureau and conversations with Shawmut representatives. I incurred over $1,000 in hourly fees before Betty even drafted the 93A Letter.

What followed was a barrage of more inaccurate amortization schedules and arrogant letters from Shawmut's in-house attorney. He insisted that they did "nothing wrong when handling this account" yet made small monetary offers to settle. My problem with that was their monetary offer to settle still didn't fix the problem of the true balance of my loan. I felt strongly that I had a right to that information and should not be forced to take a small amount of money to go away. We compiled our formal complaint and eventually filed it at the local courthouse. Betty explained that we would probably have about six months before Discovery was due for completion, the process in which both sides are required to reveal their evidence and share information. With interviews to conduct and many various fact-finding assignments, six short months was not much time and we silently hoped for a few months more.

After Betty filed the case, Shawmut's in-house attorney called. He requested a meeting at her office within a couple of weeks. At first, the response from their attorney made me hopeful. Finally, I thought –someone will give this problem the attention it needs. When the Shawmut lawyers arrived for the meeting though, it became clear that they were not interested in working the problem out. Their interest was in stopping me from being vocal about Shawmut's conduct—or rather Shawmut's *mis*conduct.

My attorney was a young, petite and attractive woman who was just starting out in her practice. Her office contained two rooms. It was a cramped but workable space and had a small window overlooking a parking lot from the conference room. Though nice and clean, it was undeniably small. After entering the multi-use conference room, my bank's attorneys instantaneously broke into a discussion of how their offices were on the 34th floor in Boston. They fluffed their feathers and strutted about importantly, telling us that we had no idea what we would be up against if we didn't close this matter and sign an agreement stating that I would never again discuss the merits of the case. They demanded complete silence about the matter in my personal circles, in public and especially with the media.

"Furthermore", nobody can figure out what exactly it is you owe. We suggest that we pick an amount and you pick an amount. Then we'll settle on a number in the middle and call it square."

The shear audacity! I immediately refused.

"Look, your client has the fiduciary duty to take care of my mortgage and further, if I didn't agree with that offer a year or two ago –why on earth would I agree to it now after incurring legal expenses?" I was stunned at their bullying, intimidations and total lack of respect—and I told them so.

"In fact, you now have succeeded in making my resolve even stronger that the court system is the only avenue left and nothing will deter me from my day in court. *Nothing!* Let's let everyone know about Shawmut's accounting practices!

Shawmut's lawyers countered, "If you do that, we will be forced to bring down the weight of our entire corporate law firm, as opposed to just using the standard in-house attorneys."

All the men looked smug as they sat in their expensive dark suits.

"Once we do that, it will be *pedal to the metal.*" They continued their belittlement by explaining how we wouldn't stand a chance against them. A strong vision of my case's resemblance to the meeting of David and Goliath came to my mind and would reappear repeatedly in the coming months.

Through my outrage, our meeting continued and the Shawmut attorneys worked relentlessly to paint their grim picture to Betty. "You won't be able to keep up with the paperwork in this case. We'll send it by the truckload. You're out of your league even attempting to take this case," one of the men said with a toothy smile.

"Have you handled corporate cases before?" another asked. "You don't think this might be too much for you?" After the numerous negative remarks, arrogance, and general disregard, one of the Shawmut Lawyers finally said, "See you in court!" And they were gone.

True to their word, within a day or two of the meeting with Shawmut's attorneys, poor Betty received a large box via Federal Express. It was filled with various requests for Discovery—interrogatories, requests for medical information, copies of statements, cancelled checks and much more. Shawmut's corporate law firm obviously was trying, and to a large degree succeeding, in backing up their threats to establish proof that Betty –was out of her league.

I think for the first time Betty realized what I had been dealing with. She now fully comprehended the lawyers' arrogance yet still never anticipated how bad things were about to turn. "Our next step is to go to court and file an 'Emergency Motion to Make Mortgage Payments Directly into an Escrow Fund' so you no longer need to make payments directly to them," she explained to me. She paced back and forth with an immediacy that showed she knew the depths they would go to intimidate us both.

"Yes. Why should I keep submitting mortgage payments to a bank that has admitted they don't know how to calculate what the true balance is?" This idea seemed easy enough and I was sure the judge would understand the clear need for this measure of protection.

In her zeal to get before the Judge I soon found out that Betty neglected to send the appropriate notification and memorandum of law in support of the motion to the defendants. They verbally attacked her in front of the judge for her conduct and represented to the court that she was in violation of the Rules of Civil Procedure. As brutal as their tirade was, it was not enough for them. They continued berating her and questioning her abilities as an attorney. The judge finally let Betty speak. She tried her best to explain to the court that her actions were not meant to be discourteous (as they claimed) nor was she shirking her responsibility. She apologized to the Defendant and the court for her tardiness in faxing them her supporting documentation. She also explained why we felt it was necessary for my payments to be placed in escrow until Shawmut could account for the payments already made, referring often to the material in our original complaint.

Then, something important happened. The judge grew impatient and suddenly appeared to be incensed at the chain of events that lead us to his courtroom and the state of disarray my mortgage was in. He wanted to see an end to this nightmare as much as I did. I should have been happy that our case was convincing when he said, *"This mess has been transpiring for far too long and it is going to end."* However, his way of ending the matter was devastating. Our original end date of Discovery was not until late June of 1995, he shaved off six months of time that we so desperately needed and announced that Discovery would now end on December 16th, just weeks away. I knew we wouldn't be able to complete their paperwork in time. Plus, I knew we would be so busy responding to their truckload of requests for Discovery documents, we wouldn't have time to send our own necessary requests for Discovery material to the defendants. *What had the Judge just done to me?*

It was clear by the look on Betty's face that she was in shock. I, however, was in tears. I will never forget what happened next. Betty turned to me in the hallway outside the courtroom doors with a look of exhaustion on her face. "Denise," she said. "I am not a litigation lawyer. You will need to find another attorney."

At this point I had already paid her thousands of dollars in hourly fees and I didn't have the money, time, strength or patience to bring another attorney up to speed. The entire situation had turned into my worst nightmare. I had gone through three years of this miserable battle and put my life on hold for too long and paid too many personal consequences. *How would I have time or money to get another attorney involved?* I remember crying all night and most of the next day. My frustrations, anxiety and fears all came out in a stream of tears followed by stomach pains and heart palpitations. The stress and anxiety were making me physically ill.

Betty called me the next morning.

"Denise, I am so sorry about yesterday but we need to find another attorney to get involved." My heart perked up slightly when she said <u>we</u>.

"I will assist whatever way I can, for free." She explained that she felt very badly because her inexperience proved costly and had only exacerbated my many problems. To prove to me her serious intentions and need for her to remove herself as my attorney, she faxed me a copy of an overnight letter she received from the Defendant's attorney containing further reprimands reciting they found her to be "discourteous, and in direct violation of the Rules of Civil Procedure." It went on to say, "You should know that if similar conduct continues in the future, we will have no choice but to bring such behavior to the attention of the court—again." I could see she was frightened and they were right. She was not up to taking on this case, not a Goliath like Shawmut and their corporate attorneys! She was not in their league—not even in the same ball park! But she wasn't malicious or arrogant as they were, she was just inexperienced.

After a desperate search, I finally found an attorney who offered to review the complaint and supporting documents, speak with Betty and make a decision how or if he could help. After he and Betty spoke, he called me in to meet with him. He explained that because Discovery time was nearing the end and very little had been done, he thought the best option we had was for him to travel to Boston, with Betty, and meet with the Shawmut attorneys in order to come to a settlement. In other words, he wouldn't take the case to court. My remaining Discovery days were at a minimum and I had powerful corporate attorneys still sending mountains of paper work and requests for material. These lawyers knew what they were doing and we were in way over our heads, just as their obvious strategy and predictions of failure promised.

As I began my meetings with my new lawyer, Joe Grover, I began to wonder to myself just whose side he was on. He didn't want to go to court, as I so desperately wanted. Rather, he thought that through opening discussion and negotiations, we could come to a resolution. I was emotionally drained and disturbed beyond belief that he wouldn't explain to the judge what happened and request the Discovery date to be extended. Needless to say, I wasn't happy with his attitude but I had nowhere else to turn. Joe and Betty left for Boston. He called to inform me that Shawmut had made an offer of settling for $7,000 to be applied toward my mortgage payoff. This was completely unacceptable. I explained to Joe that their meager amount would barely cover any of the attorney fees that Shawmut was solely responsible for and, even worse, what about the money they owe me from their accounting errors? It would still leave me with the problem that brought us all here in the first place—"<u>What</u> is the true and accurate balance of my mortgage?"

Again, the lawyers asked me to agree to a number in the middle. I told my attorney I would accept nothing less than Shawmut making my mortgage right. If they didn't have the ability to do so, then they needed to discharge the loan. I also made them aware that I would be testifying before the Massachusetts Banking Committee in support of our proposed Bill regarding the need for monthly statements and the banning of payment coupon books. There was bound to be more negative publicity for Shawmut. "Pass that on to them," I insisted.

That small snippet of information seemed to get them more willing to listen. It hadn't been my attorney that compelled them to listen—it was their fear of negative publicity and perhaps their fears of having to provide all of us with monthly statements. Joe sounded like he just wanted this to end and I just wanted it to end too, but I didn't want to be taken advantage of. I felt as if I was being condescended to and taken advantage of at every turn over the last three years. I had clearly been ignored long enough and became even more set on getting reimbursed for my attorney fees and finding the true balance of my mortgage. I just wanted what I deemed fair, nothing more and nothing less.

My attorney called back with another offer.

"Denise, you need to accept that this is probably the best you're going to get. You should take it before you end up with nothing." I felt I was fighting my own attorney—the one who I was paying hourly—and I was acutely aware that his bill was growing. I was only asking them to take care of their accounting mistakes and show me an accurate accounting.

I made it clear to Joe on the phone that I wouldn't give in. "If Shawmut can't prove they have correctly calculated the balance due on my mortgage, then they need to discharge it. It is their duty to take care of their customer's money because their customers presume accurate accounting methods are in place." Joe was unhappy with my stand, and let me know that he considered my demand to be "crazy." He became very annoyed with my position and stood by his belief that Shawmut would never agree to such a demand. I again insisted that he had to present my demand to them.

Finally, Joe called back with an attitude of surprise and a little less haughty. "They're going to do it –discharge your mortgage! You just need to pay them about $5,000 and they will discharge the mortgage balance of around $28,000. This became a point of contention between me and Joe because I felt as thought I had to fight with Joe all along the way and push him to get to this latest offer. I felt he disregarded me as Shawmut had done for years. I knew Shawmut, their lawyers and their settlement couldn't take away all the trauma, frustrations and anxiety they had put me through. I did, however, want the settlement to prove, as a matter of principal, that the bank was responsible for the errors in my account. If the bank couldn't fix their errors and find the true balance, then they should discharge it. To me it was that simple.

Joe refused to proceed any further.

"Accept this offer or find someone else to represent you and risk getting nothing. You either take what they offer or you stand to loose everything because you will not be prepared for court just around the corner." Even though I felt helpless, betrayed and defeated, I begrudgingly had to face the reality that I might have done all I could.

Once we had agreed to the terms, a Settlement Agreement had to be drafted; one that Shawmut insisted on drafting and including a confidentiality clause, forbidding me to even mention their name. When they said *confidential*, they meant *confidential*. Their need to shut me up and sweep their accounting problems under the proverbial rug just increased my already seething resentment. The Shawmut lawyers made it clear that they were only discharging my loan in exchange for my silence. There was no mistaking that. They not only wanted the amount we settled on to be confidential—they insisted on a clause that stated if I were to speak to anyone about the merits of this case (*meaning any details of the entire previous three years*) I would be fined $2,500 per instance. Additionally, if I spoke to any reporters or involved any media, the fine would jump to $10,000 per occurrence. That's *per instance* if I spoke to anyone or relayed any of the events from January 1992 through December 1994, the date of the Settlement Agreement. But as it turned out, this nightmare was far from over and their actions would forever cause the obligatory "gag" Agreement to become nullified.

I was due to speak on the merits of Senate Bill 1 feared doing so when forced to adhere to their rules ᴏᴏ secrecy. How could I do so without bringing up the circumstances of what I had been through? I asked my attorney, who said, "Go and speak, but stick to basics of why we need statements and not what happened to you. They <u>will</u> come after you. They want you quieted so much so that they bound me in the same way as you. I have to adhere to the same terms and consequences of speaking to any member of the media, or my colleagues."

I felt like Shawmut's confidentiality clause was taking away my right to heal. By taking away my voice, they were bottling all my moral outrage and fiery spirit inside of me. I didn't know how to move forward if I couldn't let my pain out and use it to make life better for someone else. Agreeing to Shawmut's terms took away my right to use my experience, life lessons and the knowledge gained in the last three years to help others. I felt that by allowing myself to be silenced, I was letting a huge number of people down. I was going to lose my freedom of speech with the stroke of a pen.

As a last-ditch effort to get something in return for this difficult silence, I told my attorney I wanted a reciprocal damages clause in the settlement. If Shawmut, or anyone associated with this case, were to damage my credit or me in any way they too would be fined. He argued up and down that Shawmut would never go for it and that there was no need for such a "ridiculous" clause to be inserted. At least that's how he saw it. "You are no longer a customer of their bank" he argued. "After all the trouble you caused in the media, they never want to hear your name again."

Despite his claims, I was more determined than ever that I needed a stipulation in the paperwork that guaranteed Shawmut would be held responsible if they adversely effected my credit in any way. Further, if they did, they would be paying attorneys fees and any damages resulting from their actions.

"You might just blow the whole deal with your demands. There is no need for you to push for that clause,"

Joe insisted. I didn't care. Again, it was partially the principle, but also partially my well-reasoned distrust of everyone involved in the case, including my own attorney. Finally, after making it clear that I would not sign anything without that specific clause inserted, Joe relented. He soon called me back with news, saying, "It's a go. They agreed to put that in just to get rid of you."

Both sides of the case rushed for the terms to be drawn up and signed because the hearing was just days away. The day after the terms were hashed out, my husband and I met in Joe's office to sign the documents, pay the $5,000 and pick up the Discharge of Mortgage. Joe immediately recorded the Discharge in the Franklin County Registry of Deeds, December 18, 1994.

The matter was settled and sighs of relief were audible on all sides. The entire confidentiality clause—to never discuss the events that led up to this settlement or the settlement itself—still bothered me. Shawmut wanted—no, they *needed*—everything to quiet down. They were not going to be so lucky, though. Confidentiality clause or not, things were about to get even more public.

Chapter Lesson: Know Your Alphabet Soup

Be your best advocate. Trust your gut and hire the right attorney. An attorney that has the necessary experience and crucial knowledge of our consumer protection laws is vital. Even with an attorney, however, consumers need to recognize that when it comes to our credit, consumer protection laws, and rights to privacy, we are powerless if we don't have the necessary knowledge to protect ourselves. In other words, if a consumer wants to fight the system, he has to know the system and that means being well-acquainted with your Alphabet Soup. What follows is a list of a few organizations, laws, and other acronyms that a consumer should become acquainted with.

- **CRA** (Credit Reporting Agency): An abbreviation that refers to the companies that calculate and distribute credit scores. The "big three" CRAs are Experian, Trans Union, and Equifax.

- **ECOA** (Equal Credit Opportunity Act): A federal law that requires lenders and other creditors to make credit equally available without discrimination based on race, color, religion, national origin, age, sex, marital status or receipt of income from public assistance programs. ECOA mandates that all consumers are given an equal chance to obtain credit. This doesn't mean all consumers who apply for credit get it: Factors such as income, expenses, debt, and credit history are considerations for creditworthiness.

- **FACTA** or Fact Act (Fair and Accurate Credit Transaction Act): Enacted in 2003, this act added new sections to the federal Fair Credit Reporting Act that were *intended* primarily to help consumers fight the growing crime of identity theft *but* FACTA seriously obstructs a consumer's rights by mandating preemption of stronger state credit and privacy laws. Provides consumers with a right to a free annual credit report. (an "every twelve months" right - If you get a free report in March 2005, you are eligible for another beginning in March 2006)

- **FCBA** (Fair Credit Billing Act): Applies only to disputes about "billing." Provides for the prompt correction of errors on open-end credit accounts (such as credit cards, revolving charge accounts, and overdraft checking) and protects consumers' credit ratings while they are settling disputes. Under this law, if a consumer is disputing a charge, creditors cannot report the consumer's account as delinquent. Consumers who question an item are responsible for notifying the creditor in writing within 60 days of receiving the bill. The creditor must acknowledge the notice within 30 days and may not do anything to damage the consumer's credit rating while the item is in dispute.

- **FCRA** (Fair Credit Reporting Act): This act protects consumers by requiring credit reporting agencies to adopt reasonable procedures regarding confidentiality, accuracy and proper dissemination of data. Consumers also have the right to dispute inaccuracies and receive a free copy of their credit report (if they have been denied credit and the consumer requests the copy within 30 days of the denial).

- **FDCPA** (Fair Debt Collection Practices Act): This act outlines the ways in which creditors can, and cannot, collect debt from consumers.

- **FTC** (Federal Trade Commission): An independent department of the federal government that regulates and enforces consumer protection and proper business practices. (FTC.gov)

- **NACA** (The National Association of Consumer's Advocates): Experienced consumer attorneys that agree to only represent consumers—not the corporations that are bound by consumer protection laws. The best place to turn when seeking an experienced attorney that can take your case on a contingency basis –getting paid only if you win your case.

- **RESPA** (Real Estate Settlement Procedures Act): A consumer protection statute first passed in 1974. The purposes of RESPA are to allow consumers to become better shoppers for settlement services and to eliminate kickbacks or referral fees that unnecessarily increase the costs of certain settlement services. RESPA covers loans secured with a mortgage placed on a one-to-four family residential property. These include most purchase loans, assumptions, refinances, property improvement loans, and equity lines of credit. HUD's (U.S. Department of Housing and Urban Development) Office of RESPA and Interstate Land Sales are responsible for enforcing RESPA.

- **TILA** (Truth in Lending Act): Intended to promote the informed use of consumer credit, primarily through disclosure, though with some substantive restrictions. It requires creditors to highlight the cost of credit as a dollar amount (the finance charge) and as an annual percentage rate (the APR). TILA requires additional disclosures for a loan secured by a consumer's home, and permits consumers to rescind certain transactions that involve their principal dwelling.

- **TLPJ** (Trial Lawyers for Public Justice): A national public interest law firm dedicated to using trial lawyers' skills and resources to create a more just society. TLPJ fights for justice through precedent-setting and socially significant individual and class action litigation designed to enhance consumer and victims' rights, environmental protection and safety, civil rights and civil liberties, workers' rights and the protection of the poor and powerless. TLPJ has various litigation projects; access to justice, battling unnecessary secrecy in the courts, mandatory arbitration abuse, federal preemption of injury victims' claims, and class action abuse. TLPJ is a not-for-profit membership organization.

- **USPIRG** (United States Public Interest Research Group): The state-based PIRGs created the U.S.

PIRG in 1983 to act as watchdog for the public interest in our nation's capital. PIRGs have worked to safeguard the public interest in state capitals since 1971. U.S. PIRG is an advocate for public interest. When consumers are cheated, our natural environment is threatened, or the voices of ordinary citizens are drowned out by special interest lobbyists, U.S. PIRG speaks up and takes action. They uncover threats to public health and well-being and fight to end them, using the time-tested tools of investigative research, media exposés, grassroots organizing, advocacy and litigation. U.S. PIRG's mission is to deliver persistent, result-oriented public interest activism that protects our environment, encourages a fair, sustainable economy, and fosters responsive, democratic government.

Chapter 5 – *The Ride Continues*

Not long after the mortgage was discharged the news was filled with stories of how the "big" bank Shawmut was about to be bought-out by Fleet Bank, an even bigger multi-state financial institution. The news explained that the merger would make Fleet Bank the largest bank in New England and probably one of the top-ten largest banks in the country. There were many protests and picketing outside local Shawmut branches throughout the state. Even with the case ending, my anxiety attacks didn't. The lingering frustrations, all bottled inside of me, were relieved a little but I couldn't seem to stop feeling pain in my stomach every time I saw a Shawmut Bank/Fleet Bank merger story plastered daily all over the news.

"Just get over it," would be the words issuing over and over again from my husband's lips.

He just couldn't understand why I would have these lingering effects of anxiety, insomnia and recurrent stomach attacks. He never guessed why the entire ordeal may have had a bigger effect on me than him. The fact that I fought this battle without his assistance never occurred to him. In his world everything had remained the same. He went about his days and nights as if there hadn't ever been a problem. The only time he came to one of my many meetings with the attorneys or Shawmut was to sign the Settlement Agreement. Many family events and changes occurred over the three years I was so grossly entangled in the case and, more and more, it was obvious that the effect of Shawmut's errors weren't purely financial.

One month after settling with Shawmut, the new session of the State Senate was called to order. Senator Rosenberg phoned to apprise me of the upcoming date of the hearing regarding our proposed Bill S16. I had decided that nothing legal was stopping me from presenting the people's petitions. If questioned by the Senate committee, I would just talk about "cases I knew of," telling the Senators that while I couldn't speak to the specifics of my case, there was a clear pattern between my case and many others.

I had the passion necessary to speak out in the Senate hearing but feared Shawmut and their many lawyers would, as Joe promised, come after me. I began to think that maybe I should, when I was called upon, simply hand the Committee the petition signatures I brought with me and avoid speaking at all. I was afraid that one slip of the tongue could cause damaging repercussions, bringing Shawmut back into my life again as they tried to collect on their delineated heavy fines.

I arrived at the Commission hearing and sat in the back with my step-son, listening to the discussions of other proposed Bills. Watching the reactions of the various committee members, I soon felt very intimidated. My name was called and I walked to the podium. Quite briefly, I stated that I was dropping off the signed petitions in support of S16. I thanked the Senators and turned on my heel to sprint back to my seat.

Senator Rosenberg, knowing how fiery and vocal I was on the issue, sensed I had been scared away. He spoke up immediately, "Ms. Richardson, could I ask you a couple of questions?"

I turned back to the podium and said, "Yes."

"Could you give an example of what happens to consumers when payments are made through the use of a coupon book?"

What a perfect question! I immediately realized I *could* answer that question without getting into the specifics of my case. I just needed Senator Rosenberg's guidance to un-freeze me. All the fear to speak left me and my passion took over as the words poured out from my heart. I discoursed on misapplied escrow payments, late fees charged even when payments were made in a timely manner and the various examples of nightmare scenarios that affected many consumers who contacted me. I tried keeping the stories generic, but then Senator Rosenberg asked, "Did this happen to you directly?"

All the fear and dread came rushing back to me. I hesitantly responded, "I am not allowed to speak on the merits of my own case."

Senator Rosenberg accepted my explanation and followed up by asking, "Isn't it true that by not having a monthly statement, extra principal payments can be misapplied and consumers would never know?"

I realized in that moment how lucky I was to have Senator Rosenberg ask that question. Aware of the "gag agreement" scaring me from freely speaking, he had astutely realized I was fearful, intimidated and worse; I neglected to mention the *crucial* point—how *additional principal payments* are often misapplied causing a myriad of problems, without the homeowner's knowledge. A rush of strength came flowing over me and I suddenly couldn't shut up. I was able to articulate—and quite well—just what could happen to an innocent consumer. That was the strong point that really captured the legislators' attention.

"I better check into my own mortgage because I send in extra principal payments every month," one stunned Legislator commented.

One by one each Senator spoke about his disapproval of *payment coupon books* because many of them regularly sent in extra principal payments just as I had. Their lenders also held funds in escrow accounts. The Senators suddenly didn't feel so assured their own payments were being handled with the care they had blindly assumed and began listening much more intently.

Judging from the atmosphere of the room, I could tell that I had the Senate seeing things my way. It was a great help that prior to the hearing the legislators had all received copies of initial letter to Senator Rosenberg. They were well aware of the events that transpired regarding my mortgage and Shawmut *prior* to my signing the infamous gag Agreement. The Senators could ask me questions based on what they had read—questions based on my story—knowing they were free to ask anything they wanted to –they didn't let a "gag order" deter them from probing for the truth, they wouldn't be gagged.

The best remark of the day was made by one of the legislators to a Shawmut representative in the audience, one of the many bank lobbyists present. He said, "Mr. 'so and so,' it looks like you are going to hit the floor if you slide down in your seat any further. If I were you, I'd want to slide down in that seat too."

That pointed comment opened up the discussion even further because *they* had brought Shawmut into the discussion, not I. I couldn't get into legal difficulties because I wasn't the one who dared to utter their name. When Shawmut was asked about these types of complaints regarding paying with payment coupon books, they immediately referred to my case as being "unique." It was clearly a strategy to make it appear that these types of mistakes are rare and my situation was merely an anomaly.

Regardless of their stance, I could tell that the hearing had been beneficial to my cause. A long, detailed discussion took place and I left Boston assured that the government understood my concerns and the pressing need for a coupon book ban. The next day my local newspaper contacted me. It seemed they had reporters in the audience of the Senate hearing and they relayed that their interviews with committee members, indicated they were very sympathetic to the need for this proposed consumer protection measure and further relayed the committee's reaction was that "*this bill had merits and would not be set aside.*" I didn't call the media, they called me -yet I was very careful to make my responses to their questions very generalized. A short time later, another call came in.

The reporter asked, "How do you feel that you were able to get a mega bank like Fleet to voluntarily move to monthly statements?"

"I did?" I asked in surprise.

"Yes, Senator Rosenberg just informed us of this in an interview we did with him about your proposed bill. Here's a portion of our interview with him that we will be publishing tomorrow. According to Senator Rosenberg, *"prior to the bill coming up for a full Committee vote; all but one bank in Massachusetts foresaw the impending changes and felt pressure to offer monthly statements? The lone dissenter—Fleet Bank, who was buying out Shawmut— agreed to switch to paper statements as soon as the merger was complete, thereby eliminating mortgage coupon payment books –at least in the State of Massachusetts."*

The editorial page editor, Charles McChesney did a follow up article which I'm sure only inflamed Shawmut's disdain for me. When the article was published the headline read *"**Greenfield woman battles the big banks.**"* The next line said *"If you have a mortgage with Fleet Bank, Shawmut Bank you might want to thank Denise Richardson. The Greenfield woman helped push for changes that will require these mega-banks to let you know where your monthly payments are going."* However, the article also explained why the Committee failed to pass the bill pointing out the bill would now be unnecessary. A few days later I received a letter containing the Committee findings that read in part:

> "...As you know the Committee recommended an 'Ought not to Pass' on this matter for two reasons, the first being that most lenders already use monthly statements for billing purposes. A very small percentage still uses coupon books, namely **Shawmut and Fleet** which are merging into one mega bank. **Shawmut and Fleet are voluntarily opting to send monthly statements, making S16 an unnecessary measure.** Secondly, new Federal HUD regulations soon take effect and will apply to all lenders, meaning that mortgagees shall provide loan information to mortgagors and arrange for individual loan

consultation on request. It was felt by the Committee that the banking industry is and should be a highly regulated industry in order to protect consumers..."

Even though the bill never made it into law, something good came out of S16 for the residents of Massachusetts. Had the public outcries and media pressure not been placed on the banks and there was no proposed S16, the banks wouldn't have agreed to voluntarily switch to monthly statements. That much I was sure of. I also agreed with the Committee findings that with all the banks in the Massachusetts jurisdiction already complying, the law was unnecessary for Massachusetts and couldn't help but silently wish I had initiated a Federal Bill.

Shortly after my hearing for S16, I began to work through many of my remaining frustrations and intrusive thoughts that had been pushed into a sort of compartmentalized lock box in the deep recesses of my mind. I "self-talked"—as I often refer to the practice with my girlfriends—as a way of getting through difficult times.

"Don't let them rent any more space in your head," I kept telling myself in those quiet moments when the three year nightmare would invade my thoughts. I began weekly therapy sessions to find a way to release the pain and frustrations that would not leave me. In all facets of life, the more a person keeps things bottled up, the more those issues come out in unwanted and incomprehensible ways. It seemed to me that it was both difficult and damaging to keep the pain inside yet that is what the Shawmut Agreement called for: a total, all inclusive "gag." My therapy sessions soon began to ease the pain of keeping things bottled up. I felt safe in that small room lit only with a coffee table lamp and no windows to see the outside. My therapist assured me that whatever was on my mind could be said in total confidence and my sessions were strictly confidential. I felt as if my healing process had begun.

It was beginning to grow dreary outside. Eleven months had passed since we discharged the Shawmut mortgage and the trees, that just a month ago were filled with bright yellow, red and orange shapes, were now bare. The leaves had died and fallen to the ground. It was turning dark much earlier and the cold northern air had been blowing in from Canada all day. It was now November and winter was about to settle in for a very long stay. I started a fire in the wood stove and grabbed a book to settle down on the couch for the night. My husband had gone out and the house was quiet.

My peace was abruptly interrupted by the phone ringing. "Is Mr. Richardson there?" I heard a man's voice on the other end inquire.

"No he isn't. Can I take a message?" I asked.

"Are you his wife?"

"Yes," I replied.

"This is Scott Lambert with Shawmut Bank and I'm calling to advise you," he nonchalantly said, "that we are calling in your mortgage due to the last three month's non-payment."

I nearly dropped the phone. Even now, I remember the flush of blood on my face as if it were yesterday. I managed to get out the words, "We don't owe you anything! Can I have your name, number, supervisor's name and the department you are in?" I scrambled for a pen. He complied and rambled off all the information I asked of him. I then flew into a tirade of what I had been through with his bank. I told him the date the discharge was recorded and that he had no right to be calling me.

"Well, we can't just take your word for that. We will need proof," he sneered.

"Oh, I will have my attorney send you proof first thing tomorrow morning." My hands were shaking and my heart was racing as I hung up the phone. How could they be doing this to me? What right did they have to call and intrude on my life again? They should have proof, why do they need more?

The next morning, fearing that my world was going to crash in again, I opted to make my first call to Senator Rosenberg. At the time, Senator Rosenberg was the Chairman of the Massachusetts Banking Commission and knew all too well what I had gone through at the hands of this bank. I relayed to him my prior evening's distressing telephone conversation with Shawmut.

"This is unacceptable and beyond comprehension. After all you have been through they continue to have an accounting problem on a mortgage discharged 11 months ago?" he snapped back.

He was clearly as incensed as I was about the matter. "That is unacceptable. Denise, let me call the Legislative Banking Liaison to see if he can help in getting this straightened out—immediately. I will call you back shortly."

With that he hung up. His incredulity that this could be happening afforded me a sense of relief and validation that my anger was legitimate. Senator Rosenberg called me back very quickly after speaking with the Legislative Banking Liaison to inform me that Shawmut had asked the Liaison for time to review the matter. *Off to research, research, research...*

"I told him that was unacceptable," the compassionate senator said.

"They've had enough time. I am to leave the country today Denise, and I let him know that I wanted to be assured this is cleared up prior to my leaving. I asked them to give this top priority. I also asked them to send to you a notification in writing from Shawmut indicating it was their error and to additionally send a letter to the three big credit bureaus in case these errors were reported to them."

I thanked him immensely, wished him a safe trip and told him I would let him know if I didn't receive the letter they promised to send.

A few days after my discussion with the Senator I received a letter from Mr. Stephen Lemony. Mr. Lemony, just eleven months earlier had been involved in the handling of my account and was fully aware that the mortgage was discharged, meaning that I owed no money at all to Shawmut Bank. The letter stated that the bank was correcting their error and adjusting their computers to reflect the change. They openly admitted that the problem was due to their error and they were forwarding notices to all appropriate credit bureaus. The letter was short and to the point yet still left a gnawing feeling in my stomach. I immediately filed it for safekeeping. *Could this finally put to rest any discussion of Shawmut in my life ever again?*

A couple of months had gone by and the news of the Shawmut and Fleet merger grew to be a controversial hot topic reported daily in the local news. The news of the merger also brought about daily protests of disgruntled consumers and worried employees who chose to picket outside various bank branches. The merger would create a Mega-bank –making Fleet the largest bank in New England and one of the largest in the country. I cringed *every time* I heard their name. We were overdue for a much needed vacation and decided that we'd take a trip to Florida. It was May 1995, approximately five months after receiving the letter from Shawmut that *promised* all had been cleared up— again. We were in Florida and Jeff, my husband's son, explained that he was having difficulty getting a car loan with a decent interest rate because he had just recently moved to Florida and had no undeniable job stability. My husband agreed to co-sign the loan for him and went to look at vehicles. Jeff found a car he liked. My husband negotiated a fair price with the salesman and completed the necessary paperwork. The sales representative disappeared for a few moments then returned with a look of concern on his face.

"You have exceptional credit, Mr. Richardson," he said. "Yet, unfortunately your Equifax report reflects a Mortgage Write-off."

My husband immediately called to give me the news. When I heard those chilling words "Mortgage Write-off," my stomach dropped and my throat closed. I could barely hear over the rapid beating of my panicked heart. I spoke to the salesman, trying not to take out my disgust and frustrations on him. It was difficult. I was tired of explaining myself without being allowed to tell the *real* reasons why a phantom mortgage write-off would appear on our credit reports due to the ridiculous "gag order" they held us to.

I stated emphatically, "we never had a write-off. In fact, our mortgage was *paid off* and discharged in December 1994." Much to our relief, their credit check *only* produced this derogatory information on the Equifax report and was not contained in the other bureaus' (Experian & Trans Union) reports –at least not then. The dealership would accept our explanation and proceed with the loan. However, due to the derogatory Equifax report, they would have to offer a loan at a "slightly" higher interest rate. I couldn't enjoy the rest of the supposedly calming vacation. Rather I was filled with intruding thoughts of returning home, jumping back on the not-so-merry-go-round, contacting the bank and ascertaining how and why this Mortgage Write-off was on our credit report. I didn't want our vacation ruined, but with that load of worry on my mind, it was.

"I thought you took care of this?" my husband said with such condescension. "Now my credit is being ruined, all because *someone* couldn't get it right."

I knew he was frustrated but I was literally sick to my stomach. I felt all the events of the past flooding into my mind at once as if someone had opened a dam. The last day in Florida we hardly spoke. I think my husband was either afraid to bring the problem up to me or he thought he had said enough. I wasn't talking because my mind was engulfed in Shawmut and contemplation of what could possibly be next. What would be the effects of my next encounter with them?" Salt had definitely been poured into my open wounds.

As soon as we returned I contacted the bank to explain what happened in Florida. They transferred me to Mrs. Bialanti, who asked, "Are you a write-off?"

"No," I told her. "We are innocent people who paid off our mortgage, which was discharged in December 1994.

Apparently, someone in Shawmut reported to the credit bureaus that we are a "write-off", but that's *not* the case."

This woman attempted to explain that they were now known as Fleet Bank and that some minor errors may have occurred during the transition. I cut her off.

"Further," I said, "whether you are now called Shawmut or Fleet, you still have the same system and same employees. Only the name has been changed, or so the news reports continue to state."

She immediately referred me to John Wasik in the Recovery Department where I again rehashed my complicated situation. There was a moment of dead silence on the phone. Eventually, Wasik said, "Let me check into this and I will call you back in 15 minutes."

He returned my call but with a very noticeable change to his demeanor. He had a very angry tone and with an arrogant voice he sharply said, "I will need a number to fax you a Universal Data Form indicating 'bank error' and 'paid as agreed.'"

He continued to relay that this data form was the universally known form creditors utilize to notify the credit bureaus of erroneously reported data. I gave him my number and heard a click in the phone—he had hung up. The fax arrived with a cover letter that said they were faxing this form to all three credit bureaus: Experian, Equifax and Trans Union. When I reviewed the Universal Data Form, I realized that it only corrected my information and made no mention of my husband's credit. I dialed the dreaded number again. I reached an angry and obviously irritated Mr. Wasik.

"Mr. Wasik, in reviewing the Data Form, it only refers to correcting my credit report and not my husband's. Could you fax me a corrected form indicating the need to correct both names?" I inquired, trying not to sound too annoyed.

He abruptly and agitatedly replied, "Fine." The phone was again hung up very abruptly. I remember feeling quite perplexed at his attitude because I felt I was being extremely patient with their continual costly errors.

I followed up my phone call by contacting each of the credit bureaus, requesting copies of our credit reports. A few weeks later they arrived. I sat in amazement while I read the report. There on paper, in plain black and white: "Mortgage Write-off—creditor, Fleet Bank." The fear, anger and frustrations re-emerged as my heart pounded.

I completed the required dispute forms and wrote a letter detailing my proof, enclosing both the Universal Data Forms and a copy of my Discharge of Mortgage, advising them that Fleet had bought out Shawmut so the mortgage Fleet was reporting –was one in the same. With my dispute letters and the Bank's Universal Data forms all supplied to the credit bureaus, I again naively felt assured their errors would be corrected. All they had to do was the investigation required of them by law. Right?

I had no real reason to believe the credit bureaus wouldn't correct the errors reported in my file. At least I didn't at this point. When I did mention to someone that I feared more battles may be on the horizon, they responded, "Don't worry. They all have the proof. There is nothing to fear. It is put to bed; you need to let it go and move on. Get over it." *Don't worry, worry, worry . . .*

Chapter Lesson: A System Flawed

Scary and ominous as it may sound, it is a proven fact that these mystery-filled credit scores, which determine which path our lives follow, are often incorrect. Inaccurate credit information can be placed on a consumer's credit report at any time. These errors include misapplied payments, manufactured late fees, medical billing errors, impermissible inquires, escrow accounting errors, and even the mixing of two different consumers' credit histories. You may be paying for someone else's mistakes without your knowledge! Remembering the theory that knowledge is power, every consumer must review monthly loan statements for mortgages, cars and even student loans. If a consumer fails to review a monthly accounting of his payments for errors, he may forfeit his right to his "true" identity.

Prior to the recent explosion of Identity Theft, U.S. PIRG (United States Public Interest Research Group) collected 200 surveys in 2004 from adults in 30 states who reviewed their credit reports for accuracy. Key findings included:

- Twenty-five percent (25%) of the credit reports contained errors serious enough to result in the denial of credit;

- Seventy-nine percent (79%) of the credit reports contained mistakes of some kind;

- Fifty-four percent (54%) of the credit reports contained personal demographic identifying information that was misspelled, long-outdated, belonged to a stranger, or was otherwise incorrect;

- Thirty percent (30%) of the credit reports contained credit accounts that had been closed by the consumer but incorrectly remained listed as open;

Oftentimes consumers are unaware their credit has been erroneously altered until they attempt to refinance or purchase a new home or car. Worse yet, they find they have been paying additional insurance premiums and higher interest rates unknowingly for years, making it too late to recover the money lost, due to that inaccurate score. It's important to realize that a theft of identity can erupt in your life at any time and it isn't always the "typical" criminal that is the thief of your true credit identity.

Chapter 6 – *CrediTerrors*

My daughter was having car problems. We had put a lot of money into repairing her car considering it was not in the greatest condition in the first place. After our trusted mechanic gave us a large estimate for the repairs needed to get her back on the road, we had to admit that it was time to get her a new vehicle. Considering that we had co-signed a car loan for Jeff, we felt it only fair to do the same for Jadie. It was the spring of 1997 and my husband and Jadie visited various car dealerships on a mission to find her a dependable car that she also considered "sporty" enough for her taste. They found a car that she fell in love with and negotiated a price. The car deal included an undercoating treatment, which meant she couldn't drive away with her car that day. They promised she could pick it up in just a couple of days. Excitedly, she waited for them to call her.

When the call finally came two days later, which to her seemed like a lifetime, she came to me in tears.

"Mom, the car dealer says I can't get the car! They said it has something to do with your credit!"

I grabbed the phone out of her hand. "Hello? This is Denise, Jadie's mom. What is going on?"

"Mrs. Richardson?" a man's voice questioned.

"Yes, please tell me why my daughter is standing here in tears."

"This is the Auto Mall. I am so sorry but we can't obtain the loan for your daughter because when the finance department ran a credit check on your husband they found a Mortgage Write-off."

I was livid, but conveyed to him to the best of my limited ability (being aware I was "gagged" by the bank) that our mortgage was paid. There never was a write-off. I asked him if I could fax him the documentation to prove what I was claiming.

"Yes, please do. I will take it to my boss and see what we can do," he said.

I immediately faxed a copy of the Universal Data Form, supplied over a year ago by Mr. Wasik, the letter from December 1995 that indicated it was bank error, and a copy of the recorded Mortgage Discharge. As soon as the fax was sent, I contacted Mr. Wasik at the bank.

It was quite apparent that he remembered me because he copped the same rude and hostile attitude he presented the prior year. The moment I told him my name, he flew into a rage.

"I have already sent you copies of the Universal Data Form that I sent to the credit bureaus for both you and your husband. It is not *our fault* you are being denied credit and, furthermore, we have wiped your name out of our system. As far as the bank is concerned, you are on your own. We *never* want to hear your name again. Do not contact me again." His words ran on in an angry stream.

The phone rang almost immediately after Mr. Wasik hung up on me. It was the Auto Mall.

"Mrs. Richardson, my boss looked at your documents and, if we can contact Mr. Wasik at the Bank to confirm these are authentic, we may be able to process the loan."

I supplied him with Mr. Wasik's telephone number, but I warned him that he was not at all in a very good mood. "Please call me back after you speak with him," I asked.

A short time later, they fulfilled that promise. They explained, "Mrs. Richardson, Mr. Wasik did verify the information and GMAC has agreed, under these circumstances, to honor their acceptance of your loan request. We can now move forward."

What should have been a simple transaction that ended with my daughter enjoying her new car had turned into another ordeal of humiliation and embarrassment. I had gone through another frustrating confrontation with Mr. Wasik, who yet again blamed me for something I was powerless to control. By now, I knew what the situation foretold—more hours of requesting credit reports and more hours of written disputes, providing everyone and their boss with my documented proof, then finally requesting that the three bureaus correct our credit reports.

I eventually wrote for and received a copy of the TRW (now known as Experian) credit report and all indications were that the derogatory information had in fact been deleted. The report appropriately indicated the Shawmut Mortgage had been "paid as agreed" with all payments made on time and, furthermore, was discharged in 1994. What a sense of relief. They cleared up our credit and all signs indicated smooth sailing. No more Mr. Wasik, no more writing letters of dispute and no more frustrations. It was right there on paper—"Paid as agreed"—the best I could get. Finally, there was no citing of a "Mortgage Write-off" anywhere on their report.

I was cautiously optimistic that this time they "got it" and my credit reports would reflect the excellent credit rating I deserved. Yet, on what appeared to be an average Tuesday morning, I heard my office door swing open. I looked up and there was my husband with a very annoyed look on his face I knew immediately –something was up.

"Hey...I just got a letter in the mail from BP Gas. I applied for a BP gas credit card (for both of us) because they were offering free gas coupons if I opened an account with them. I thought this was a good deal because that's where we both buy our gas. Guess what the letter says?"

"What?" I asked.

"Turned down on the basis of a Mortgage Write-off," he said. He angrily dropped the papers on my desk and stormed back out as if I were the one who turned down his request for credit.

I sat there in my office, stunned with disbelief. Honestly, I wondered, where's the camera? This must be some sort of a joke. How could this keep happening to us? When was it ever going to be safe to apply for something as little as a BP gas credit card without fear of rejection? I didn't care that Mr. Wasik had told me never to contact him again. I needed to find out why they were reporting this information to the credit bureaus when last time I checked it had been removed from our credit reports. Mr. Wasik was the only man to answer these questions.

I called the bank and asked for Mr. Wasik. When I was asked who was calling, I had no choice but to reveal my name. A voice came back on the phone and said he wasn't available—she would leave him a message. I again contacted the credit bureaus requesting copies of our credit reports.

What I received back in the mail immediately brought tears to my eyes. I found that not only had the bank *re-reported* the false information and the credit bureaus had re-inserted it, but now there was an *additional* "Mortgage Write-off." The erroneous report now reflected I had two Mortgage Write-offs, both containing their own separate account numbers. One account number was identical to the number on the account for the mortgage we discharged in 1994. The other reported *Mortgage Write-off* had what appeared to be a bright and shiny new account number, one I had never seen before. It seemed they unconsciously—or as I would later suspect, intentionally—had inserted this reference along with *alleged dates* in 1996 they claimed 90-day late payments were made—March 1996: 90 days late and October 1996: 90 days late. How was non-payment of a non-existent debt possible? And who had made the alleged payments in 1996? Not me. That was years after our mortgage was discharged. I refuted the information and another investigation began.

One ordinary day, my husband appeared at my office door.

"What's up?" I asked.

Without an immediate response, he walked over to me and dropped a small stack of papers out of his hands onto my desk –and turned to leave.

"What's wrong?"

"You'll see," he said, and with that he left the room.

I opened the first letter. It was from Experian. There was a copy of my credit report and a letter indicating the results of their investigation. It read, *"After our investigation with the furnisher, the furnisher reports the information to be correct. We will continue to report the following account as indicated on the enclosed credit report."*

As I looked over the credit report, I found Experian had removed the *duplicate* mortgage write-off, which contained a different account number, but had "verified" the other write-off containing 90-day late payments made in 1996 (and now 1997!) on the report. This is the result of their investigation? These errors were now verified as accurate? Who the hell was making payments on a discharged loan – certainly not me? I really believe that unless you live through chronic long term frustrations that you have no control of –it is difficult to really understand the effects on your psyche- you feel as though you must be crazy.

Before my eyes welled up, blurring my vision entirely, I opened the other letters my husband gave me, which were the findings of Trans Union and Equifax. Trans Union had forwarded a copy of our credit report which indicated that the Mortgage Write-off had been deleted. Equifax however, was a different story: *"Equifax has completed its investigation of the accounts you disputed. We have verified with the creditor that the account you disputed is accurate."*

There it was as big as life again—a Mortgage Write-off to Fleet Bank with all the 90-day late payments erroneously listed *–and* verified as accurate! They didn't even place a notice of dispute on the report. They did, however, report various dates for mysterious and *verified* 90 day late payments. Hmmm?!

Who verified this? Who on earth would have the authority and the evidence to make this imaginary write-off exist? I realized in that moment that the only possible "furnisher" of that information was Fleet. Out of complete frustration, I contacted Equifax by telephone and demanded copies of their purported "investigation." I needed the names of the people who verified the erroneous information. I wanted the facts and the all-important paperwork that would help me prove that Fleet was intentionally violating the terms of our Settlement Agreement not to "adversely affect" our credit. Remember that "ridiculous" little clause that Joe thought was an unnecessary demand of mine?

Equifax agreed to send the dispute back to investigations and to send the results in the mail.

In an effort to cover all my bases, I contacted Fleet again and left a message for Mr. Wasik. I wanted the Universal data forms resubmitted to the credit bureaus with a copy sent to me so I could see for myself it was done. I reminded him of our Settlement Agreement, in which they promised to never adversely affect my credit rating. He begrudgingly agreed but with the caveat that this would be his last time trying to assist me or speaking to me in any way. He let me know just how much it would upset him to even hear my name again. Knowing the anguish I felt each time I heard their name, it was mildly relieving to know that a not-so-innocent person would go into spasm when hearing my name as well.

My head was spinning so fast from this credit carnival ride that in my stress, I nearly freaked out every time the phone rang. I remember one particular afternoon, when that telephone of terror was answered by my husband. "Hello?" I heard him say into the phone as I headed toward the house from the driveway. "No, I don't owe anybody," he vehemently stated. "Alright, send the proof. I am telling you right now, I don't have a mortgage with Fleet. I never did."

He chose his words carefully, not disclosing any of the reasons for this nightmare having fears of being heavily fined.

"I had a mortgage with Shawmut and the mortgage was discharged in December, 1994. If you say I owe something please send me the proof in writing."

Hearing only one side of this conversation, my feet ran as fast as they could into the living room where he stood with the phone up to his ear.

"Who is that and *now* what do they want from us?"

"This woman, Ms. Freda, is telling us they are going to put a lien on our house because they bought our loan from Fleet. She says we now owe over $21,800 plus accrued interest," Bob explained, as much in disbelief as I was.

"She's with Portfolio Recovery Associates. They purchased this debt."

"Ask her if they paid money for this supposed debt we owe," I yelled.

"Yes, she said they bought it from Fleet."

"Tell her they bought a non-existent debt from Fleet and they better go get their money back," I was furious and simultaneously floored by the incredible incompetence that must be at play.

He repeated what I said. He added, "Okay, send it in writing," and hung up.

"How was it left?"

"She said she would have to contact Fleet and obtain the original mortgage documents with our signatures on them. Then she would forward the papers to us. She also said she would note the file accordingly."

This was not comforting news. *I'll have to send your file to research* and *you should receive something in the mail in a few days* was commonplace to us now. It seemed all we could do was brace for the worst.

A week or so passed and we received a demand letter in the mail from Portfolio Recovery Associates. It stated that they purchased our mortgage debt from Fleet Bank and they were demanding over $21,800 plus accrued interest. I was angry, frightened, and sick to my stomach again. There seemed no end in site and I felt exhausted from all the frustration. Once again I obtained copies of our credit reports and waited in fear to see what they contained. Could this Portfolio collection account now be on our reports? Knowing how the system worked, I disputed their demand letter both by telephone and in writing, forwarding all the pertinent information the CRAs needed to see we were innocent.

Ms. Freda contacted me again a month later. She was actually calling to ask me what arrangements I could make to send in payments before they placed a lien on our home. I reminded her of our last conversation, when we had asked for written proof before they took any action, which she admitted remembering.

"We never received any proof that we owed anything—no mortgage—no note—no proof," I said.

"I'll have to check with my supervisor, Mrs. Richardson, because I do see here in the notes on your account that we requested verification from Fleet in September and they have not yet responded."

I couldn't believe my ears.

"How can you threaten to put a lien on my home when you haven't received any proof or validation from Fleet? Also, you are in violation of the FCRA and the Fair Debt Collection Practices Act because you are calling me *again* on a debt that I sent documentation to you proving I don't owe you anything –and you have no verification stating otherwise."

"I'm sorry Mrs. Richardson, I will look into this," and she hung up.

Approximately a week later, we received another claim notice from Ms. Freda demanding payment. This time the letter was even more threatening, clearly spelling out that the collection agency was going to pursue "any available remedies to collect this debt." The notice additionally stated, *"You have failed to respond to our attempts to contact you."* This was an outright lie. Not only had we contacted them by telephone and writing, we had just spoken with a representative two days prior to this demand. What did they want us to do?

I immediately contacted Ms. Freda and asked her how this could be happening. More importantly, I asked, "Why does it state that I had not been in contact? We both know I have."

"Hmmm. I don't know why it says that. I know I talked with you and it is noted in the computer that you called. The computer does make note of your dispute as well." She seemed more confused about everything than I was. My frustration at the blatant ignorance and incompetence of the system was growing with every conversation I had with creditors.

"I did request a *second* investigation from the furnisher because the bank never responded to the first request," she finally said, as if this were her only route of action.

"Have they responded to your second request? Obviously not within the required time limits imposed on them by law," I replied.

"No, it doesn't look like they have responded to either request. That is, not yet," she added, as if she truly believed they would. "If what you are telling me is true, Mrs. Richardson, we should not be calling you. In fact, we should not be reporting this to the credit bureaus either."

"You mean you did?!" I could not contain my anger at this point. I was fuming—all the work, the copies, the faxes, the phone calls, all in vain.

"Even after we told you we didn't owe this money, you took it upon yourselves to destroy my credit with a collection account for a non-existent debt?" I couldn't help sounding upset—there was no hiding it. I was angry, frustrated and felt I had every right to be.

Back then I was unknowledgeable and just beginning to learn how the *unfair* credit industry works. I had no idea that the moment we received that first call –it meant they *already* reported their newly acquired debt. This fury turned to sheer terror when I received new credit reports. Portfolio Recovery Associates was now listed on them as "**bad debt, in collections.**" Even worse, however, there were the Mortgage Write-offs again. There they were, for the world to see, clearly re-inserted into our account. We now had two Mortgage Write-offs and a collection account. I would say it illustrated unequivocally that Fleet was, in fact, "adversely affecting my credit" and the problems were being compounded.

Our lives were again becoming totally disrupted. I was taking anti-anxiety prescriptions just to help me get through the overwhelming fright that would strike me every time I contemplated this would never end. I deteriorated to the point where I felt knots in my stomach just seeing Fleet commercials on television or riding past a Fleet Bank branch. I developed a nervous condition where I would pick at and bite around the base of my nails so badly they often bled. My stomach attacks were back full force and I found it difficult, if not impossible to sleep through the night. Our credit reports were full of inaccuracies and our prior excellent credit "grade" had plummeted to 9. Though a high credit "score" is a good thing, the credit "grade" assigned to each account is a number between one and nine, a one being the best you can get and a 9 being the worst.

A trusted friend advised me, "Why don't you go back to the attorney you had in 1994? Have him do something to stop this! Under the FCRA, they are not allowed to re-insert erroneous, previously corrected information, nor could they continue to reflect ninety day late payments on a loan that didn't exist."

All of a sudden it was as if a thousand lights were turned on. Maybe due to the stress or being physically sick, I had forgotten about that dreaded Settlement Agreement and yelled out, "The clause, the clause!" I remembered the clause –the one that I vehemently fought to have inserted into the Settlement Agreement. That agreement had silenced me and I hated its very existence. Could it now benefit me? It stated very clearly that they (Shawmut and their successors) "had not and would never adversely affect" my credit. Further, if they did, they would be responsible for all legal fees incurred in my defending my rights.

There was my answer to stop the not-so-merry-go-round that was whirling away my peace of mind yet again. Energized by this realization, I completed all the necessary paperwork to dispute the information with the credit bureaus yet again, but this time was different. This time, I believed, would be the last. I would now dump it on their lap to repair their errors by bringing that all important clause to the attention of the bank's legal team.

My first call was to Joe, the attorney who insisted unequivocally, that I never needed to worry about them bothering me again. Of course, I knew better as the past is often a good predictor of the future. I remembered how he thought I was being paranoid and obstinate in not agreeing to sign without putting their promise to leave me alone in writing.

"Joe, guess what?" I asked, feeling a little smug that I had been proven right. "Since 1994 when we signed that agreement, I have been fighting with Shawmut and Fleet in correcting derogatory information they have been reporting to the credit bureaus! Remember how you told me I didn't need that clause to protect me, the one that stated Shawmut would never adversely affect my credit? Well, now it turns out it could be the only way to stop their continued harassment because it appears they are in breach of that Agreement."

"Come over to my office tomorrow Denise, and bring all the documents you are talking about."

I met with Joe the next day. I brought a copy of the FCRA which I had already reviewed –I even highlighted the pertinent statutes I felt the bank and credit bureaus were clearly violating. I showed him where false information had been deleted then re-inserted. I conveyed to him that it seemed no matter what precautions my husband and I took, we could not get the bank and the credit bureaus to stop disseminating this false information. Joe told me to leave the copies of my letters, credit reports and the FCRA with him and he would review everything. He phoned me the next day.

"Denise I reviewed the FCRA and all your documents. In my view, you cannot hold Fleet in breach of the Settlement Agreement because your dispute is with the credit bureaus," Joe explained. "Fleet had put them on notice with the Universal Data Form. You need to dispute the information with the credit bureaus to see where this information was derived from. In my view of the FCRA, consumers can't sue the furnishers of information."

This was not the enthusiastic response I was hoping Joe would give me. He continued, "I can't send Fleet a letter telling them they are in breach of the Agreement when I don't believe they are." Two days later I received a bill for his services...$480 for his *mistaken* opinion.

His astonishing interpretation of both my Settlement Agreement and the FCRA, I would later find to be grossly false. The furnishers *can* be sued under the FCRA and heavily fined by the state and federal enforcement agencies for failure to re-investigate or for failure to have "reasonable procedures" in place to ensure that false credit data doesn't land on a consumer's credit report. At the time, however, I had no idea Joe was completely wrong. I trusted in his assessment but that didn't mean I was going to give up.

Emotionally and physically drained, I did everything and anything I could think of to solve my inaccurate credit problems. I contacted both the Attorney General's Office and the Federal Trade Commission to report the actions of all corporations involved. After explaining my situation, as they did with the Shawmut mess, they told to contact an attorney because neither governmental office would handle individual complaints. They only step in when they see a clear pattern of abuse affecting many consumers. But I contacted them anyway to report these corporations' abusive actions. I was desperately seeking someone—anyone, to help.

I saw the courtroom doors ahead of me, about to swing wide open again. But –what I didn't know, was that I was about to, as they say, *make a federal case out of it!*

In a bid for support, I again turned to the public and the community of other victims whose stories could prove I wasn't an anomaly. I knew I was still "gagged" and couldn't disclose any information about the battle with Shawmut but I could talk about this new battle to stop inaccurate credit reporting that was transpiring with Fleet. I would just skip over the "merits" of the Shawmut nightmare and speak of my current inability to stop Fleet and the credit bureaus from reporting and disseminating false credit information. I couldn't help but think that if I spoke out and spoke loud enough, they would take action to correct their errors as they did in the past. All I ever wanted was the return of my accurate credit rating–accurate data—and to be left alone. That was what I deserved and what I was promised. I wasn't asking for anything more, but I wasn't going to accept anything less.

Chapter Lesson: Using a Magnifying Glass

Every consumer should feel a twang of fear about the accuracy of their credit reports. Not all derogatory information is easy to spot when examining a report. Here is a list of common problems that every consumer needs to look for when "monitoring their credit files with a magnifying glass."

- **Check the dates of derogatory notations**: When there is <u>no</u> date, the credit scoring software will probably substitute the last time the account was reported to the bureaus. That process is called "ageing" and is illegal because it affects the length of time the data can be reported on your file. Derogatory data such as collections must come off your file after seven years. If a disputed collection, such as a bill from March 1, 2002 was reported erroneously as March 1, 2005, that means the account could be reported an additional three years due to inaccurately aged data.

- **Check the open/closed status of accounts:** Consumers often complain that their report contains old charge-offs, reported as current and open delinquent accounts. That is in direct violation of the FCRA and can be costly to you.

- **Make sure accounts are closed correctly**: Upon closing an account, request that it be notated *"closed at the request of the consumer."* A closed account can affect your score if it is notated as "account closed by creditor" because it appears that the creditor closed your account for a possibly problematic cause, which also affects your credit score.

- **Be careful utilizing consumer credit counseling and debt negotiating firms:** These firms often have excessive fees and can hurt a credit rating. Long after a debt is paid, notations reflecting "consumer credit counseling" can remain on the file and it's extremely difficult to remove these types of derogatory notations.

- **Common problems with disputes:** Dispute letters should always be sent via certified mail and copies kept—forever! However, the CRAs have 30 days to complete their investigation. If the creditor does <u>not</u> verify the disputed data, it has to be deleted. If it is verified, they can refuse to reinvestigate subsequent "frivolous" disputes, but must provide details about that verification. Many times creditors verify incorrect data. In that case, contact the creditor directly and demand account verification, providing documentation proving innocence.

- **Dispute Statements:** By law consumers are entitled to a 100-word consumer dispute statement, which is often recommended by "credit experts." However, this statement will not help consumers get a better interest rate or insurance premium. Creditors rely heavily on your score and don't have the capability to override that score by a notation of dispute. Even worse, the inaccurate data could be removed while the statement remains. Creditors such as landlords and mortgage underwriters, who receive the entire report, could be alerted to a possible problem simply by reading your statement. It can do more harm than good.

- **Inquiries**: Every time a creditor seeks information, their inquiry is noted on the credit report and most of these inquiries stay on reports for two years. However, only inquiries during the previous 12 months can lower a credit score.

- **Additional notations:**

  o **PRM** – A promotional inquiry in which only the name and address were given to a credit grantor for solicitations. PRM inquiries remain on file for 12 months.

  o **AM or AR** – These inquiries indicate a periodic review of your credit history by one of your creditors AM and AR inquiries remain on file for 12 months.

  o **EQUIFAX, ACIS or UPDATE** – These inquiries indicate Equifax's activity in response to consumer contact with them for either a copy of your credit file or a request for research.

  o **PRM, AM, AR, INQ, EQUIFAX, ACIS and** UPDATE inquiries do not appear on consumer reports that creditors receive, only on copies provided to the consumer.

- **Shopping around**: Additionally, the scoring system is supposed to only count auto inquires and mortgage inquires made within a time frame of 30 days as one inquiry. In addition, the system keeps track of 12 months of inquires and any cluster of such inquires from mortgage or automotive lenders within a 2 week period will only be counted as a single inquiry. The intent is to allow consumers to shop around for the best rates by giving them time to make better deals without being punished with a lower score due to multiple inquires. This is how it is supposed to work but things don't always turn out the way they are supposed to. Often, consumers must take action to have this policy benefit them personally.

- **Adverse Action:** Adverse action occurs when your interest rate or availability of credit is increased, denied, cancelled, or adversely changed due to information on your credit report. This may include car insurance, home insurance, car loans, home loans, car leasing, cell phone, etc. It was once standard (prior to the FACT Act) that a consumer would only receive an "Adverse Action Notice" if he was denied credit. However, now consumers are to receive an "Adverse Action Notice" letter anytime that they do not receive the most favorable rates or service based on what data is in their credit file. It is of utmost importance that every consumer inquires as to what the best rate available is in advance. That way, you will know that your "deserved" credit may have been re-rated based on what could be an error in your report. It is very important to get this adverse action letter if, in fact, your score is the basis for an increased premium or interest rate.

Additionally, and very importantly, this information will be of no help if a consumer doesn't have documentation. Consumers must save all records, letters, copies of correspondence and credit reports indefinitely. It is also a good idea to keep a journal of conversations, contact information and records of all pertinent information. In the world of credit reporting or debt collections, remember: you are often guilty until proven innocent.

Chapter 7 – *Names May Hurt –*
But Numbers Kill

The prospect of returning through those courtroom doors seemed daunting. Finding an attorney that could fight for my rights was an overwhelming thought in itself. My stamina was failing and I knew I needed to find the strength to move forward, find an attorney that could go through my mountainous paperwork, and actually understand and *get it.* Yet everywhere I turned, it seemed no one had any help to offer me. Even Joe had thrown up his hands, saying that there was nothing he could do. His opinion seemed like yet another betrayal in my fight for what I thought was right. This would not be the last act of betrayal in my life but the exhaustive years of chronic stress began wearing on my health and well-being; something these corporations place little value on.

While overly stressed out during my ride on the not-so-merry-go-round, I had often noticed my heart beating rapidly. I visited my doctor, who watched me closely while I wore a heart monitor for a time. After completing a stress test and seeing a cardiologist, my doctors felt confident that I had tachycardia—stress induced arrhythmia. When I was initially given their diagnosis, I didn't agree with or believe them. I was frightened and felt sure they were missing something. One of the few things I had learned about my biological father was he had died at the age of 51 from a heart attack. Surely these heart palpitations were an indication of something heart related, not stress related. However, I soon began to see the pattern of my own symptoms and understood that stress does not always produce physical effects immediately, but those effects can emerge after chronic emotional and mental frustration.

I realized that during those frustrating times when I battled Shawmut, fighting for my true credit identity, my nights were sleepless. Oftentimes, I had found myself pacing around the house at night, walking in circles, thinking about the sense of powerlessness I had. I would question myself, *how could this have happened? Why couldn't anyone hear me?* I had to take prescriptions to fall asleep, prescriptions to stop heartburn, prescriptions and hospital trips for bouts of stomach pain, and prescriptions for anxiety-all attributed to stress. I had endured almost every test out there to rule out pancreatitis, kidney disease, and gallbladder or stomach cancer. You name it—they tested me for it.

On one specifically painful night, I was raced to the hospital unable to catch my breath. I experienced a very rapid heart beat and then, I soon passed out. The emergency room staff tried to tell me it was a panic attack, but I felt sure that I was suffering a massive heart attack. *It can't be a panic attack without some mental trigger,* I thought. I had just finished having dinner at a restaurant when suddenly the room started to spin and appear to black out on me. As I struggled to make it to the restroom, I passed out. Where was the "panic" in a dinner out, I wondered. Could this too be the product of stress, which could hit my body out of the blue – at anytime?

The stress induced arrhythmia, and my newly diagnosed panic attack, were forcing me to think that the doctors *might* be right about my health issues being related to my nerve-racking confrontations with Shawmut in the past and my new battle that brought them all crashing back into my life. What I learned about my frequent stomach attacks only solidified that belief. My doctor diagnosed the condition with three little letters—"IBS."

"What?" I asked, thinking I didn't hear him correctly.

"You have a very bad case of IBS."

Again, a terrible acronym was invading my life I thought.

"What's that?" I asked.

"Irritable Bowel Syndrome," he explained.

IBS is a very debilitating disease as anyone who suffers with the painful and life-altering condition will tell you. It is life-altering because you no longer feel safe and assured that you can fly on a plane, go to a concert or any other event that might keep you a distance from the privacy of your own bathroom. You never know when an attack is going to come on, which makes you hyperconscious of the location of the nearest restroom at any given moment. IBS is not curable and is triggered and exacerbated by ongoing stress.

I was forced to realize that the doctors were right. Their test results kept coming up negative and I had to take what they were telling me about the effects of chronic stress, much more seriously. I had to get the anxiety out of my life but felt I had little to no power to do so.

The anxiety was understandable considering how much I had been through. I'm sure I spoke to every customer service representative that ever touched a phone trying in vain to "fix" it before I was forced into a courtroom battle—both times. I took names, dates, and extension numbers. I showed my documentation to everyone that I could convince to review it. It seemed as if nothing I did could stop the impending lawsuit that I had hoped would just go away, once they corrected their errors and took accountability.

Where could I turn when the bank said it wasn't their problem, the credit reporting agency said it wasn't their fault either and I knew the problem wasn't caused by anything that I did? Nevertheless, I had no power to stop it from happening. Worse, nobody cared. I began to reach out to the public and the on-line communities of other victims who offered both empathy and encouragement. I became an avid follower of these on-line consumer communities which was a surprisingly large group of people. They all had stories just like, or worse than, my own. In fact, I remember my jaw dropping open when I found myself on a consumer-friendly online forum that had logged nearly 400,000 posts from victims of inaccurate credit reporting and/or collection company harassment. One site alone had over 10,000 members and many "guests" that visited this site on a regular basis. I was stunned.

They were of all genders, races, states and financial standing, but had all fallen victim to the arrogance and negligence of some sort of mega-corporation. Some of the people had already lost their homes, some hadn't. Some grew weary of the fight and gave up, while others were still embroiled in their own personal nightmare. It was a community dedicated to giving hope to the hopeless. It was a group that knew what such a *David and Goliath* fight could do to a victim's life but it was also a community that had found strength in each other.

I reached out to them to share my story. I was still "gagged" and couldn't disclose any information about the battle with Shawmut, but I could talk about my current battles with Fleet. An initial letter I wrote to this online community unexpectedly seemed to contain a piece of nearly everyone else's misery, which unpredictably made my story relatable to those who read it. Innumerable letters of encouragement and stories of heartbreak began to fill my email daily. Soon I started getting letters from the media and other consumer advocate web sites all requesting interviews or seeking to publish my initial accounting of my story to help shine a light on how far a consumer must go to clean up credit reporting errors. Consumer Aid and Education Center published my letter and labeled it "A Consumer's Nightmare." Without these online forums, letters of encouragement support and the sympathetic ear they provided me, I don't think I would have had the strength to endure the upcoming battle –that by now I recognized was looming on the horizon.

While I initially logged onto such sites for research and direction on where to turn next, I never imagined that my story, written out of desperation, would be so relatable to so many other victims. I had gone through years of feeling trapped by a sense of helplessness and I didn't think anyone could ever understand. Clearly, I was mistaken. As I browsed the internet, talking to other victims and learning of their own similar nightmares, I sadly became aware of so many who suffered far worse than I—people who lost their homes, their jobs, and their families. Post after post, story after story, would refer to families dealing with pain and lawsuits, frustrations or losses they suffered at the hands of the credit bureaus and various creditors that ignored their pleas for help—their legitimate complaints and requests for help continued to fall on deaf ears. They too were seeking that allusive validation, help, understanding and guidance as I was. I was not alone. Not only did I find support and encouragement, all validating my exhaustion and the anxiety that had taken over my life, but I found people who knew how I felt and even better –They *got it*.

I would respond to consumers on these post boards, convey my troubles, offer them an ear, and soon found it was becoming a type of therapy that I desperately needed. I would head to my computer with a coffee in hand each morning to find hundreds of letters in my email. It seems my letter allowed them to realize that someone else knew how they felt and was willing to speak out. I responded personally to each one, whether it was to thank them for their kind words of encouragement or offering the same kindness and support their letters provided me.

To illustrate a glimpse of typical letters that were arriving daily, I have included a few condensed snippets here.

> To: DeniseRichardson@*****.com
> From: Consumer@*****.com

> Hi, Denise. I read about your story on the credit website. I went/am going through the same thing. My wife left me when we lost our house. Even if I can ever settle with the bank, they can't give me my marriage back.

> To: DeniseRichardson@*****.com
> From: Citizen@*****.com

I just saw your letter and the trouble that you are going through. I feel terrible for you. I went through the same thing with my bank five years ago. Eventually we settled, but I almost lost my home in the process. My husband and I haven't been the same. If there is anything I can do to help you, let me know.

To: DeniseRichardson@*****.com
From: Someoneelse@*****.com

Dear Denise,
I wish I had read about your experiences before I talked to my bank. They gave me almost the exact advice your bank gave you. I have been fighting them for seven years now. My wife gave up on it after we lost our house in 1992. Even without the house, I'm still trying to fix my credit. Your story is a tragic inspiration. God Bless!

To: DeniseRichardson@*****.com
From: Bankvictim@*****.com

Denise,
I can't believe what you went through. I just started into this mess. My bank is giving me the run around. I have already talked to 15 different customer service reps and not a single one could give me a real answer. I am overwhelmed trying to work this out on my own. Any advice or help would be much appreciated.

To: DeniseRichardson@*****.com

From: Anewfrined@*****.com

Dear Ms. Richardson,
My prayers are with you. We all need to stick together through these troubles. As long as we are together, the good will prevail. I am sending a copy of your story to my Congressman.

To: DeniseRichardson@*****.com
From: Consumer@****.com

My heart goes out to you. You are fighting for all of us. I couldn't take it anymore and gave up fighting but only after I lost my home, my marriage and my health. Please find the strength to keep fighting for all of us who weren't strong enough.

To: DeniseRichardson@*****.com
From: Someonelse@*****.com

I am going through a lawsuit too. Maybe we can trade information and documentation to help each other. My attorney is ********. Maybe your attorney would like to contact him?

To: DeniseRichardson@*****.com
From: Helpcry@*****.com

Thank you for your efforts. Can you help me? I am going through the same thing and found I can't refinance due to inaccurate credit information that has gone on for 5 years. My wife took the kids to her mother's house to get away from it all. At least the bank won't try to take them too. I am desperate and need to talk to somebody.

These countless letters became my source of inspiration and strength, and offered me a calming sense of security that would strengthen my spirit, kind of like a child's "security blanket." As a child, we knew that logically that little blanket we held on to so tightly, carrying it everywhere, wasn't capable of protecting us from evil. However, it certainly provided us with as much comfort as a true source of protection. These letters would validate me and that validation was priceless. Some letters were hung near my computer so I could look up at them for continued inspiration when I felt most vulnerable and ready to give up. This was one of those letters my eyes would often turn up to and one that I drew particular inspiration from...

From: Erin Brockovich
To: Denise Richardson
Date: Monday, April 17, 2000
Subject: Way to go!

Denise: Thanks so much for writing and sending this website information. I will be sure to look it up. It sounds like you have had quite a fight on your hands. It's people like us though, who will always make a difference. I am inspired – way to go!

Best Regards,
Erin Brockovich-Ellis

In the beginning of my struggle, I was fully willing to admit that what happened probably started as just an innocent bank or computer error. That is, until I found there were so many victims and the true magnitude and scope of the problem became crystallized. As a result, almost accidentally, I grew into a consumer advocate and wrote consumer editorials for Consumer Aid and Education Center that was a non-profit website run by a long time advocate named Barbara Woodcox. She had found me through the initial letter of desperation I wrote to Kristy Welch, founder of www.creditinfocenter.com. Kristy had contacted me to ask if they could use my story in a feature article they planned to entitle, *"Who is Ultimately Responsible for Correctly Reporting Your Credit History."* Kristy thought my original letter sent to her site painted a human face on the extraordinary lengths one must go through when faced with inaccurate credit. I was, by the time I received her letter, then in the beginning stages of filing a lawsuit and immediately checked with my attorney. He gave me his approval to let her print it and was as unaware as I was then, that this letter would rally other consumers, grab the media's attention and with it –the defendants' wrath.

Who is ultimately responsible for correctly reporting your credit history?

The scary way an innocent consumer got burned by her mortgage company

We have been paying higher interest rates on our current credit cards due to their errors and can not obtain nor consolidate to a lower interest rate loan or credit card until they correct and notify all companies and credit bureaus involved.

Our only option now is forced litigation against the bank, Collection Company and the three credit bureaus. I should not be forced into expensive litigation and endure their acts of defamation when we are innocent consumers that have done nothing wrong. We are trying to gain the attention of our legislators to correct the laws that were created to protect us from the effects of inaccurate credit reporting and hold furnishers accountable for their willful and negligent actions that ruin our reputations. The FCRA says we can sue credit bureaus but not the furnishers, yet it is the furnishers that provide and report the inaccurate information. The Credit Bureaus blame the banks and the banks blame the credit bureaus and the consumers are put in the position of having to prove their innocence and defend their destroyed reputations.

The congressional purpose of the FCRA is to protect us from this egregious behavior yet they take away our access to the courts and our right to sue "furnishers". The FCRA should, at the very least, delineate penalties and fines when they do not adhere to the regulations. We are totally innocent yet we have to now endure long, expensive litigation against 5 large corporations just to receive what all consumers should expect and deserve . . . accurate credit reporting.

I am committed to changing the FCRA by getting Congress to hear the pleas of the consumers and to raise consumer awareness to the injustice of the Fair Credit Reporting Act. If you can help me with this endeavor, I would be very grateful.

As I received countless letters, I became more incensed at the lack of consumer protection laws that had any real teeth. I also learned many consumers were barred from the doors of justice due to what was at the time, a little known clause secretly contained in many credit card agreements and mortgages, which mandated consumers to utilize arbitrators to settle any disagreements that could arise.

When I first heard of the practice of waiving a consumers right to access to the courts I was outraged and in disbelief. "Isn't that unconstitutional?" At the time, the late 90s, it had just begun to spread and consumers would only find out about it if they had a problem, sought legal counsel, or threatened to sue. Only then, the creditor would point out the hidden small print in their particular contract which basically said, *you can't sue us* and *you must use an arbitrator—at your expense—and, oh yes, come to where we are located at your expense.* I researched how this practice was allowed to grow and quickly found that it was quickly becoming another major obstacle thrown in the path of unsuspecting consumers when simply trying to hold someone accountable and find justice. I wrote to an attorney I found on the web who was leading the fight against hidden mandatory arbitration clauses that in the 90's were just beginning to blossom. F. Paul Bland is a notable staff attorney with Trial Lawyers for Public Justice, a public interest non-profit organization whose main projects and cases center on protecting consumer rights and setting crucial precedent setting case law. He's the kind of attorney everyone would want representing them. He's extremely knowledgeable, conversant and really cares about consumers who have been wronged. He spent time answering my questions and sent me additional articles he had written to help answer my burning question, "How can this be Constitutional?" Apparently, forced binding arbitration is viewed as Constitutional because, simply by signing a contract or using a credit card, wherein the creditor demands BMA, (binding mandatory arbitration) then essentially you are agreeing to waive your right to sue by using that credit card or signing that contract or loan document. After reading his many articles, I became more upset at the fact that forced BMA was being touted as a consumer protection tool, a way to save a consumer the hassles and expense of a courtroom. In actuality it was far from being a "tool" for consumers –it was just another, purposely false, twist of the real facts-something they do often –and are quite good at.

I began to understand why these corporations set their sites on making binding mandatory arbitration the norm as opposed to consumers having their day in court. Essentially, BMA secretively sweeps settlements under the rug. There is no case law, there is no judge or jury of our peers, but instead an arbitrator, usually a retired judge, who hears both sides of the story and makes a decision that is confidential and binding to both parties. I couldn't help but wonder where I would be if I didn't have access to the courtroom. What about all the people who wrote me with no place to turn? I began researching this latest anti-consumer measure and was shocked to find it was continuing to grow – at alarming rates. If binding arbitration is accepted by both parties –then fine. But –we should have a *choice* to accept that avenue to settle disputes. It shouldn't be snuck into fine print documents *without* the consumer's knowledge.

Deep inside the fine print among the information pamphlets we receive, are often hidden clauses that specifically bar you from suing your credit card company, insurance company, bank, car dealer or even your friendly computer maker.

Banks, insurance companies, credit card issuers, computer manufacturers and car dealers began inserting fine print into their contracts, service agreements, and invoices that *waives the consumer's right to sue them in court for any reason.* (This includes both individual suits and class actions). Instead of filing a lawsuit, *the consumer is required to submit all disputes to an arbitrator that is <u>hired by the company</u>, and the consumer is expected to pay the arbitrator's fee!*

Waiving our right to sue is just another way corporations place themselves above the laws that are created and intended to protect us. By taking away our right to access to the courts, they don't have to worry about their wrongs being exposed. As a result, if they don't adhere to governmental regulations-who will know about it? Access to the courts is our most effective means of holding companies accountable for their actions and forcing them to adhere to state and federal consumer protection laws. Forced binding arbitration does not afford us vital and relevant case law that deters them from heaping their same abuses on others.

Without large fines and penalties delineated for their negligence or recklessness, and without consumer access to the courts, WHAT is their incentive to be responsible? What will force them to take effective measures to ensure that our disputes will be handled without the expense and duress of utilizing the arbitrator of their choice? There is no trail of case law created for the victim that walks behind you – that is the real power they take away from us and the real reason they want to take away our rights of access to the courts.

Often times consumers can't afford, either financially or emotionally, to take on these large corporations, but to specifically *deny* consumers their right to participate in a class action or a private right of action *if they seek to* — is unconscionable.

If this practice is allowed to continue, when will it stop? What if all the products we purchase such as food, medicine, toys, etc., included a small print clause on the package (or inside the package) saying, "You are signing away your right to sue us simply by purchasing this item?!" Think about it! If creditors and car companies can take away our right to sue because we purchased their services, *how long will it be before pharmaceutical companies can poison us and toy manufacturers can injure our children without fear of being sued for their negligence?* Again –let me say **I'm not advocating lawsuits!** Consumers have always been on the short end of the stick when it comes to a level playing field – but we were always assured that we had our Constitutional Rights intact and have the ability to turn to our courts. Often a consumer going to court to seek justice is strengthened with the knowledge that if they win their case – their case law can make a difference in helping others. Through mandatory arbitration though – the results of the arbitrator's decision remains veiled in secrecy and is of no use to the next consumer who walks through the revolving door. Isn't that in direct opposition to what our judicial system is about?

When I began speaking out on the dangers of binding mandatory arbitration, I was soon inundated with letters from consumers who, just as I predicted, were as unaware of this latest anti-consumer action as I once was. Creditors of all sorts were beginning to incorporate these "you can't sue me" clauses into their respective agreements and/or contracts without the consumer's knowledge—until the consumer learned about it when a problem arose. Soon Barbara Woodcox contacted me and asked if I wanted to become a contributing editor on her site at Consumer Aid and Education Center and respond to consumer complaints, questions and issues while writing articles pertinent to consumers. It was a valuable opportunity that would provide me an avenue to speak out about consumer issues I was passionate about. I could continue to raise awareness and offer a sympathetic ear to those that desperately needed one. I had simply, almost accidentally, grown into a consumer advocate the same way anyone does when dealing with a misfortune, tragedy or one of life's many hardships that sparks the necessary activism to effect change. Sometimes something hits you so hard that you're very being is altered – you're not the same and moreover, you have an undeniable aspiration to stop it from happening to others.

When I realized the overwhelming amount of people suffering from all types of consumer problems, most due to negligence, malicious intent or corruption, I learned just how gaping the loopholes in our consumer protection laws really are. I knew that unless I walked back through those courtroom doors, I wouldn't find that accountability, deterrence and validation that so many of us needed. I knew I needed to fight using my personal nightmare to establish clear case law. I couldn't give up and let them destroy my credit identity and couldn't let all those consumers that I promised to fight for down. I realized my case was no longer just about me –it had become important to all of us who deserved to be heard.

However, the corporations I was dealing with, along with their corporate attorneys, didn't view my attitude in quite that light.

Chapter Lesson: Web Resources for Consumers

When a consumer has an issue, they are usually the "small fry" fighting against the "big cheese" or "big cheeses" of corporations or agencies that have harmed them in some way. The Internet is a vast resource for such consumers in terms of educating themselves and finding out their next course of action. Speak out and tell your story. To that effect, I would like to share some of my favorite consumer-oriented websites with you.

For a wealth of information regarding debt collection issues, sample dispute letters, links and crucial updates consumers can turn to Bud Hibbs at www.budhibbs.com. His book *Innocent Until Proven Guilty* is also available at that site for free download. Bud Hibbs has helped millions of consumers with collection problems and is a regular guest on the *Ernie Brown Show* (KRLD 1080 AM) in North Texas. He is an accomplished author of *The American Credit System: Guilty! Until Proven Innocent*" and *Stop It! A Consumer's Guide to Stopping Collection Agency Harassment.* A veteran of radio and television, he has been featured on Phil Donahue, Oprah Winfrey, CNN Headline News, CNBC, ABC, CBS, and his own talk radio show from Dallas. Bud's site receives over 2 million visits a month.

- Autoissues.org: A site dedicated to stopping binding mandatory arbitration in the automotive industry.

- Bankrate.com: A site devoted to money handling advice and information including investments, insurance, college financing and more.

- <u>Bayhouse.com</u>: A resource forum on mortgage, credit and credit scoring tips as well as inside information on current cases.

- <u>Clarkhoward.com</u>: This talk show host offers to help consumers "save more, spend less and avoid rip-offs."

- <u>Consumerfed.org</u>: The Consumer Federation of America offers consumer information broken down by industry i.e. energy, finance, housing, or health and safety.

- <u>Consumersunion.org</u>: A non-profit publisher of consumer reports.

- <u>Cardratings.com</u>: Information, forum and resources on credit issues.

- <u>Guardmycreditfile.org</u>: American Consumer Credit Education Support Services (ACCESS) founded this website which includes news and information on credit and privacy issues. There is a special Fraud Alert section to inform users of new financial scams and a section on children's privacy, which details abuses and what we can do to protect our children.

- <u>My3cents.com</u>: A leading source of real consumer advice. Visitors come to learn, interact and voice opinions regarding companies, products and services in an open community.

- <u>Privacyrights.org</u>: A non-profit organization that offers consumer information, advocacy organizations, policy watch, and privacy tips.

- <u>Publiccitizen.org</u>: Focuses on protecting health, safety and democracy

- <u>Uspirg.org</u>: Advocacy for public interests (also see state PIRG's).

- Wjfa.net: Where's the Justice for All (WJFA) is a nonprofit organization established by activists and victims to educate journalists, elected officials, and the public that when victims are denied justice, it causes economic devastation which wreaks havoc on individuals, families, and businesses.

- Consumercity.org: A site with information about credit scores, credit cards, consumer protection laws, identity theft, current credit scams, insurance issues and informative articles with links to consumer complaint sites.

- Creditboards.com: A community of people and resources featuring a great forum that has a wealth of information, live chat, peer-to-peer help, online resources, news and credit industry alerts.

- Creditinfocenter.com: Provides information regarding consumer credit counseling, debt consolidation, bill consolidation, and rebuilding or repairing credit and even avoiding bankruptcy.

- Fight-back.us: This site is dedicated to fighting corporate fraud.

- Givemebackmyrights.com: Crucial information about the dangers of mandatory arbitration.

- Msfraud.org: A site devoted to mortgage servicing fraud, which includes an informative consumer forum and a wealth of legal information.

- Myfaircredit.com: A credit dispute site, forum and industry news, founded by consumer attorneys.

- Timduffy.com: Nationally known consumer advocate, serving and assisting consumers.

- Care2.com: An online community for people who want to make a difference. There are over 5 million members plus many different forums and causes with one common denominator—they all involved people who care striving for change.

- Givemebackmycredit.com: A site where consumers can keep informed, sign up for newsletters and help fight for stronger consumer protection laws.

- Mortgagereform.org: By guiding consumers to state and federal agencies, and various legal resources, this site features free tools and resources to run predatory lenders out of business.

- Responsiblelending.org: A resource for predatory lending opponents. The Center for Responsible Lending is fighting to stop financial abuses through legislative and policy advocacy, coalition-building, litigation, and industry research.

- Citizen.org: Public Citizen is a national, nonprofit consumer advocacy organization founded in 1971 to represent consumer interests in Congress, the executive branch and the courts.

Resources for legal information or for help in finding an attorney:

- Atla.org: The site of the Association of Trial Lawyers of America where consumers can find a lawyer, learn their rights, and access resources.

- Consumerlaw.org: The National Consumer Law Center is America's consumer law expert, helping consumers, their advocates, and public policy makers to use powerful consumer laws to build financial security and assure marketplace justice for vulnerable individuals and families.

- Naca.net: Home site of the National Association of Consumer's Advocates, a membership of attorneys who pledge to only represent consumers, not large corporations.

- <u>TLPJ.org</u>: Trial Lawyers for Public Justice is a national public interest law firm dedicated to using trial lawyers' skills and resources to create a more just society. TLPJ fights for justice through precedent-setting and socially significant individual and class action litigation.

Chapter 8 – *The Spin Cycle*

Still stinging from what I considered to be betrayal by my former attorney, I hired two new lawyers who agreed to represent me on a contingency bases (solely because of that clause I had inserted into the original Settlement Agreement with Shawmut providing for attorneys' fees). Prior to the actual filing of the lawsuit—just as we did the first time around, my new attorneys filed a Chapter 93A letter, advising the defendants (Fleet and the "big three" CRAs) of their actions, or in my case, their inactions. My attorneys underestimated my problems and believed that a simple demand notice surely would make it all just go away. They didn't know what I had learned the hard way—these corporations, their errors, and their countless attorneys don't "just go away."

In the beginning of this case, I found that I was not only fighting the corporations but fighting to get my attorneys to see the magnitude and scope of the problem at hand. I forwarded them my emails from other consumers along with various cases I had researched. I attempted to explain the mind-set I was up against when dealing with Shawmut's lawyers in the past. My attorneys only began to see the magnitude of our fight when they pried promises out of Fleet to correct their errors only to find those promises would soon be broken—to their surprise, but not mine. It wasn't long before I was a humiliated with another denial of credit, found I was paying higher interest rates than I deserved, and learned of Fleet's latest damaging methods of reporting more dirty data, even after their promises to correct their errors were made. My attorneys were soon not only surprised by these corporations' inactions to take effective measures to correct their many glaring errors, but they would also be shocked by their continued actions that further destroyed my credit rating. When they realized what I was trying so hard to convince them of—that all the promises to correct errors would be broken, many times—only then did they begin to take my continued complaints seriously.

Mine was a large and complicated case. Too many consumers were innocent victims that didn't have the financial backing or mental stamina needed to hold on and fight against one Goliath. I, on the other hand, had five of them—Richardson vs. Fleet, Equifax, Experian, Trans Union and of course the collection company, Portfolio Recovery Associates, who bought the non-existent Mortgage Write-off from Fleet. However, because Fleet sold the *non- existent* debt to the collection company, they quickly released this collector from any liability, holding them harmless, and accepted any liability directed at Portfolio.

My life quickly turned into endless days of legal research, answering interrogatories, and compiling our own necessary Discovery. This stage of the lawsuit is devoted to preparation and evidence gathering. In the Discovery phase, each party can ask questions called interrogatories and request documents that are a laundry list of everything that could possibly be utilized in the case. Each defendant had their own set of attorneys who were bombarding my two-attorney law firm with stacks of requests for both written responses and a boatload of documents. If you can imagine, it's quite an intimidating and overwhelming process that is also very cost-prohibitive. In a two attorney office, they obviously have cases that need their attention to keep the cash flow coming in to pay their bills. On the other hand, the corporate defendants and their attorneys have many hands and very deep pockets without any concern for keeping their law firms running. Unfair? Yes, absolutely and without doubt. I have learned, however, that justice is not fair or equal. There is no such thing as a fair and equal playing field when taking on mammoth corporations. Don't think those corporations don't know this—they count on it and use it to their advantage. My full-time job became helping my attorneys with drafting interrogatories, depositions, research and obtaining the necessary documents: tax returns, medical records, credit denials, credit reports—virtually every piece of paper that was connected to my family and our lives.

The pressures were mounting and my adversaries became larger than life size. They were now virtual tenants residing in my home, eating meals with me, watching television with me, working with me, following me to social events, sitting in on my doctor appointments, and even sharing my bed. There seemed to be no stopping their overwhelming intrusions into my life. My attorneys, Larry and Alan, had a small office with one secretary. Larry had assigned Alan to do 90% of the work while Larry kept the firm's business running. Alan still had other cases but the bulk of this enormous case was set squarely on his desk. This was to be Alan's first FCRA case and, knowing this, I provided Alan with as much case law as I could find. Often Alan and I would talk for hours and respond with emails daily. We had our heated moments (due to overwhelming stress) but, through it all, we grew both mutual respect and a friendship. Numerous times, Alan would relay how he would discuss my case with friends or family in disbelief of what happened and was, in fact, continuing to happen.

"I wouldn't have believed this could go on this long if I had not seen it with my own eyes. I'm as riled up and as incensed as you are."

He was very astute, proficient and best of all, there was no mistaking –he *got it*!

One of our conversations in particular struck me right between the eyes. He had just gotten off the phone with one of the defendants' attorneys. He turned to me while I was in the office at the copy machine and said, "Wow, they really don't like you. When I explain to them what you have been through their response just astonishes me."

"What makes you say that?" I asked.

"Well, I have never had a case where the other attorney actually resorts to calling names. Plus, their stand is so arrogant and without remorse. Their response is always the same . . . 'So, we screwed up. Big deal. What are her damages?' I can't stand it either Denise –but, you need to know they are going to try to get this into mediation."

"What do you mean name calling –and mediation?" I asked with a tone of both anger and disbelief.

"Well . . . comments such as 'she's just tenacious, an activist' –and oh yeah, they made a sarcastic remark to the effect of...w*ho do you think you are, 'Oprah Brockovich?*'"

I knew their sarcasm stemmed from their total disdain for my passion to both make a difference for other consumers (Oprah) and have my day in court (Brockovich) but really –how childish!

It was at that point that I remember actually understanding how arrogant my adversaries were. I had experienced some of their gross haughtiness in the first case and knew they had no remorse for what they had done to me. Yet, to hear those words that day sent me reeling because I understood the depths to which they would sink. Oprah Brockovich didn't bother me but hearing the word *mediation* did and so did their attempts to minimize what they had put me through with their arrogant stance of *Big deal. What are her damages?!*

I had been through years of abuse at their hands because they wouldn't clean my credit—credit that they themselves dirtied. My psyche felt as if it had been stuffed into a washing machine—scalded, agitated, pushed around in violent spin cycles and then hung out to dry—only to find that the process had done no good. My credit was still stained-their data was still dirty! They had hung me out to dry and there I was, stiff and tired, tattered and torn, yet all they could say was, "Big deal. What are your damages?"

My God, I uttered to myself in disbelief. Even though I could prove I was humiliated, denied credit, physically and emotionally beaten and left for dead –it didn't matter to them. I pointed to the facts, statutes and laws they were in violation of—all the evidence was on my side-yet they strategically held up their yardstick and screamed "So what – what did it *cost* you -monetarily?" Emotional scars run deep and last a lifetime but they refuse to place any value on that.

They play down the damages caused by prolonged periods of continual wash and spin cycles meant to clean their dirty laundry—my credit! The same stains were always left behind. So many consumers are put through multiple cycles and wonder, as I did, *Can I survive another turbulent wash and spin cycle?*

Creditors and the court measure consumer damages by asking: "What did it cost you in actual dollars?" I don't know how you feel, but I think most people would choose their families, sanity and good health over dollars. Yet, it is undeniable that Defendants will devalue consumer complaints, overzealously demanding that all they want to hear about and all that really matters in a courtroom, is <u>real</u> costs and <u>real</u> monetary loss. That is, if consumers can even make it to the courtroom. Of course, Defendants push towards mediation and arbitration, both of which remove the judge and jury as well as any public accounting of their heinous, willful actions against consumers.

Alan kept telling me, "Denise, they'll never want, or never probably allow this case to go to court—never!"

He believed in that strongly because I had the facts and documentation on my side.

"You're a very articulate, knowledgeable witness that a jury would accept as trustworthy and likeable. You know this case inside –and out. Of course we need to keep doing the leg work *as if* we are going to court –but we may never get there."

I couldn't believe my ears. *"As if" we were going to court?* I didn't go through all this to be forced into another gag order and Settlement Agreement which would allow them to sweep their errors (and their culpability!) under the rug, dust themselves off and start again on another innocent victim.

I realized my adversaries were looking at this as if it were a game of who could outlast the other. They were going to make my life a living hell unless and until I picked up my marbles and went home. That was not going to happen. Alan would try to calm me and, in hindsight, I think he knew we would never see a jury no matter how determined I was to see that happen. The defendants were much more powerful and much more determined to stop me from being in front of a jury.

I dismissed the prospect of settling instantly and told Alan so. "I can't believe I have gone through this for eight years, morning until night, and they not only trivialize the effects of what they have put me through, but now you're telling me they will never *want* this to go to court? *Tough.* There's just no way I will be silenced again and stopped at the courtroom doors." I was passionate about this and wanted Alan to understand how intractable I was when it came to this issue.

I continued, "I didn't ask for this—they did. I gave them countless opportunities to shut down this ride, but they only continued to exacerbate my problems. Then they have the nerve to minimize the consequences of their actions. I am not fighting just for myself here. I want case law. I have people that are counting on me."

Alan waited patiently for me to finish my diatribe. "Well," he looked at me and said, hesitating as if he was afraid of what my reaction would be, "they want to push you into mediation and the court might make us do that. So, you must try to prepare yourself for that possibility. You can have your day in court but the Judge may order attempted mediation first. Would you be willing to undergo non-binding mediation?"

After reading my story this far, I think you can imagine my reaction and response. I really didn't have the ability at that point to articulate properly how I felt about that. I do, however, remember my response quite well.

"Not fucking going to happen."

I remember those words, where I was standing and how I felt as if he said the word "mediation" to me five minutes ago. It was at that point, that very second, when I knew this was going to be a battle all the way to the end. I wasn't going to be dealing with just the defendants and their attorneys' arrogance and unfair rules of the "game." I was going to be fighting to the finish with the judicial system as well, and anyone who tried to gag me. The game was set in motion by them—I didn't want to play. Nonetheless, it was definitely in progress and now we had a judge and the justice system that would alter or enforce rules, whether I believed it to be fair play or not, or whether on an equal playing field or not.

"What is the sense of non-binding mediation Alan?" I asked. I felt they just wanted to have a "preview" of what the trial would be like. Alan agreed but said sometimes the practice could be a valuable tool and we could also get a preview of the hand they were going to play. I thought it was a huge waste of time and expense. Since they were pushing for it, how could that be a good thing for me?

Days began to run into weeks and weeks into months as the trial preparations were a constant and growing intrusion. My attorneys had taken over a room across the hall from their offices and labeled it the "war room." Inside that room were mountains of legal documents, boxes containing reams of paper encompassing years of my life, all marked by year and item—medical records, tax returns, case laws, credit reports, Discovery, complaints, for and from five major corporations. When I looked at this room and all of its contents, I couldn't help but digress to the same questions that ran through my mind for years. *How did I get here and what did I do to deserve this?* I had never missed a payment and always paid on time. Yet, there I was standing at that door, peering through the glass window, seeing my life all compartmentalized in boxes containing reams of paper. Was that really what my life had become?

Our pre-trial hearing was getting closer. It was a hearing with the judge who, I was told, would schedule various courtroom hearings, trial dates, and cutoff dates for various motions and Discovery. Larry told me there was no need for me to be there. "Oh, I'm going to be there," I said. "I want to attend and hear for myself, see for myself and watch for any trickery the defendants tried to pull." I didn't trust anyone at this point. Alan laughed, "I think it is going to be great to have you there! We can ride together. Want to pick me up?"

We walked into the courtroom and I sat quietly behind my attorneys on the right side of the court room. On the left sat the Defendants' attorneys and their entourage sat squarely behind them to my left. We all stood as the judge entered the room. He began by addressing the defendants, asking them to recite what happened and how this case got before him. Fleet's attorney stood up and began reciting his version of events nonchalantly. He said something similar to "Well, your honor, we did this . . . and then *unfortunately* we did this....and *unfortunately* we did this and *unfortunately* this happened." I don't think he had even gotten to the part where they sold the non-existent debt to a collection company when the judge heard him utter one too many "unfortunately{s}." He abruptly pushed back his chair and threw both hands in the air, straight up into thin air.

"Ms. Richardson's stress level had to be off the scales," he proclaimed. Yes, that is exactly what he said. I will never forget his exact words because at that moment I felt a piece, however small, of validation. He knew how I felt! Tears silently streamed down my face. I wasn't making any noise but my cheeks were full of tears, as if someone had turned on a water faucet. I had no control of them.

Suddenly, the judge's eyes landed on my face and quickly turned to Alan and Larry. "Is that the Plaintiff sitting behind you?" he asked.

"Yes, your honor," one of them responded.

"I would like to meet with you and your client in my chambers and then I will meet with you," he said, turning a stern eye towards the defendants' table.

While I was in chambers, the judge told me he couldn't help but notice how emotional I was. He relayed that he had hopes he could "get a number" from me that I had in mind to settle. He could take that figure to the Defendants, to see if they would accept it. I remember it only brought on more tears as I told the judge I didn't want to settle. I had no "figure" in my head. I had made it this far and I didn't understand why I couldn't have my day in court to claim both the justice and case law that could be helpful to so many other victims out there.

The judge told me I could in fact move on to trial. He was not at all forcing me to settle, but rather thought perhaps if we all spoke we could find a way to end this nightmare now and prevent more pain that would be endured in a courtroom battle. The judge left us in his chambers and went back to the courtroom to talk to the defendants and their attorneys, instructing that we were to wait there, and he would return shortly. When he returned, it was with the news that they had made an offer to settle. He told me the "number" and my attorneys thought I needed to consider it quite seriously.

I was still incredibly reluctant, to say the least, to settle but my attorneys and the judge had one other little card to lie down, and one I had never heard of before. It's known in the Federal Judicial System as Rule 68. Rule 68 basically mandates that if a defendant makes a valid, written offer of settlement and a plaintiff declines it, that plaintiff could end up being penalized for not accepting that offer. What? Why? Yep, that's the truth. You see, according to good old' Rule 68, if the defendant makes a written offer to settle, and the plaintiff doesn't accept that offer and that offer turns out to be more than what an actual jury awards, the plaintiff could then be held responsible for court costs and attorneys fees—from the date of that written offer until the date the jury trial is over. In my view, it was a sort of punishment for taking up the courts time when, if the offer was accepted, the case could have been over. All of a sudden, the case resembled a "game" not unlike poker. I felt the need to consult a good crystal ball when making this crucial, life-altering decision.

When contemplating this Rule, consumers are basically choosing whether or not they should gamble on how much the jury will award and whether that will be more than the defendant offered. This doesn't seem like a fair and equitable judicial system, it sounds more like the game show "Deal or No Deal?" What happened to *justice for all* and our

Constitutional right to a jury of our peers? It's difficult enough to get into the courtroom, to fight for case law that (*that has real teeth*) to deter companies from doing the same to others. I wanted that case law—not a secret settlement. Much like my previous Settlement Agreement, such a settlement would be secret and couldn't be used to help others by revealing their obvious pattern of abuse in any other court case. The credit and banking industries don't want case law—they would rather settle, sweep their wrongdoings under the proverbial rug and move on—without a trail of any pesky case law if they came up on the losing end. Rule 68, however, gives them a little edge. The gamble isn't on <u>their</u> money or <u>their</u> livelihood. It is on the victim's life and on that of his family.

Much to the chagrin of my husband as well as both Larry and Alan (and probably the Judge as well), I opted to move toward trial. It was a simple decision for me considering my passion about the situation, but I was betting it wasn't so simple for them to understand.

"Okay," the Judge said, "let's go out and let them know you want to move toward trial and we'll schedule your pre-trial dates for motions and Discovery."

As we all walked out of chambers and took a seat, I could clearly see the shock on their corporate faces. I found out later from Alan –they were angry. They were expecting the judge to come back to them with another offer and thought that would be the end of the matter. They heard the judge's tone and thought this would come to an end, or at least hoped it would.

We were all standing again and the judge left us to set up all the details of the pre-trail process. As we stood, I heard Fleet's attorney say, "Okay, let's get some dates set up for depositions." His dismay was quite noticeable because his face was bright red, his teeth were clenched and his tone became very intimidating. "Well, we're going to need several dates for Mrs. Richardson. Let's block off entire days and, oh yes, we will need her daughter's address as we plan to depose her. Also her therapist, Mr. Richardson and also

Ms. Richardson's primary care Doctor will have to give depositions as well." He angrily snapped the latches of his briefcase shut. He then looked at me sternly, attempting to wound, as he said, "We will be doing a motion to obtain her hard drive as well."

I kept my game face on, as if their intimidations didn't bother me and I wasn't incensed that they were threatening to use my daughter, my hard-drive and therapist as if they were weapons. As if I couldn't see they were clearly and purposely taking this hard-line stand to bully and browbeat me. His actions were saying, "You want to play hard ball? We'll play hard ball."

I sighed. This is how it's going to be, I thought, be tough and don't show them they can get to you. I smiled and said, "Great!"

Chapter Lesson: Legally Speaking

Whether you are staging your own legal battle or merely attempting to understand the system, knowing the finer points of the legal process is essential. Here is glossary of terms I have referred to.

- **Deposition:** A deposition is testimony given under oath and the penalties of perjury prior to trial. Attorneys are allowed to ask whatever they like and answers are documented by a court recorder, who types up every word spoken. Depositions can last for hours or days. Depositions can be videotaped as well. Depositions can—and are—used by one side or the other when it is time for trial.

- **Discovery**: A preliminary phase of a trial during which both sides must reveal their evidence and share information. This often includes interrogatories, requests for medical information, copies of statements, cancelled checks and much more depending on the nature of the dispute.

- **Hearsay**: A legal term used to describe a statement made out of court that is meant to support the facts of a case. Such undocumented and un-witnessed statements are considered rumor and are not usually admissible.

- **Interrogatories**: A set of written questions requested and exchanged between parties that are meant to clarify evidence and determine the facts that may be brought forth in the case.

- **Rule 68**: A civil rule dictating that if a defendant makes a valid, written offer of settlement and the plaintiff declines it, the plaintiff may be held responsible for the defendant's attorneys' fees and court costs from the date of that settlement offer (through the end of the trial) if sought by the Defendant, and agreed upon –by the Judge.

If you are undergoing a legal battle of your own, get yourself an experienced attorney or firm that can handle the financial strain you will undoubtedly be up against when pitted against deep pocket corporations and their defense team. You will need your own team of experienced consumer attorneys or at least a law firm that has the necessary staff to handle the massive paperwork. Don't underestimate the lengths defendant attorneys will go to when trying to intimidate both you and your attorney. At the least, ask whatever attorney you turn to, if he is prepared to take this on with the necessary staff and finances needed.

Chapter 9– *Beginnings and Endings*

Depositions are often considered to be very intimidating and can last for days on end, which becomes exhausting and financially draining for all involved. During our lengthy depositions, my adversaries' impatience and disdain for me grew transparent. They never tried to make niceties or even hide their contempt for me. My concern, however, turned out to be their "need" to continuously threaten to subpoena my hard drive. I knew if they gained entrance into my hard drive, they would be peering into the lives of innocent consumers, many of whom rightfully expected confidentiality when writing to me about their upcoming or ongoing lawsuits. I could not and would not allow that to happen. These threats really angered me— deposing blameless people and taking over my hard drive, were actions that could hurt innocent people –people that I cared about. Although they may have considered it a way to push my buttons, what they didn't consider was just how protective I was towards these innocent, already victimized consumers. Their threats only made me want to dig my high heels in –even deeper!

My advocacy and public speaking was also a point of contention for the defendants, who wanted to turn that passion against me. For example, in one of my depositions I remember being asked to name every person I had ever spoken to about this matter. I feared this was the prelude to my being forced to submit these letters into Discovery. It was common knowledge that I had been very vocal on the web and they were aware of various interviews I had given by nationally recognized journalists and advocates and, to put it mildly, they hated it.

My hard drive and correspondence should not be declared evidence –it had no bearing on the case, I argued, and was only a ruse to glean information about other cases from unsuspecting victims. Alan responded to their request for my listing every person I ever spoke to by saying, "Do you have all day? She can't possibly list every person she's ever talked to during the last eight years."

"Sure she can," he replied. "Just start naming them—we have all day." After Alan gave me the nod that required me to answer, I think I began mentioning nationally-recognized names and government organizations rather than those of consumers, friends and family so not to expose their identities. I also didn't want to inadvertently mention the name of a consumer who may have a case against them. Then, they could suddenly and transparently subpoena those personal and private letters. After about ten minutes, they asked to break for lunch. Alan and I left to get something to eat and discuss the morning's deposition. I was doing great, he said, and no matter how hard they tried to get me to blow up, I remembered to stay calm.

I fully expected that after lunch we were going back to my laundry list of naming all of whom I had ever spoken to over the years about this mess, (caused by their errors) but we didn't. Instead, they started on my medical history going back years and actually asked me questions such as, "Did you see your doctor for a yeast infection that you may or may not have had?" They began picking up various medical records, placing them in front of me and asking me about every visit I ever made to the doctor. It was clear they just wanted to run me down and stress me out, which I was not going to allow them to accomplish. My medical records were filled with various appointments for chronic abdominal attacks, stress-related heart arrhythmias, irritable bowel syndrome triggered by stress, insomnia and anxiety attacks all transpiring and corresponding to their intrusions. If anything, I felt very comfortable in the depositions because I had nothing to hide and had wanted for so long to tell my side and show them the effects of their abusive actions. It's like I wanted to unzip my head and pour it all out on the floor to be finally swept away. If only it were that easy. If only life were that simple.

Just as they had deposed me, we were responsible for deposing them. All parties can be present at each deposition. Yet, it is costly to travel to various states for depositions when defendants are not in your area. One of the depositions took place in Texas and Alan asked me to be available via telephone. He said I could be on speaker phone listening in and taking notes as some of the other Defendants were, and that way, if questions arose or consulting was necessary, we could speak during a break confidentially. Each time I was deposed, all attorneys were present one way or the other.

Considering this process, it is easy to see how costly the Discovery phase can become when numerous defendants have to be deposed. The bills for necessary travel expenses, transcribing expenses, court reporter expenses and the attorney fees really rack up. We found ourselves with a limited amount of money up against mega-corporations who enjoy access to unlimited funds and the necessary staff to handle the gargantuan amount of time and paperwork involved.

I also learned of another hurdle when trying to obtain Discovery from the defendants. The purpose of Discovery is exactly that—to discover pertinent information that each party has through documentation requests and depositions. The Defendants got to depose whoever they wanted, but we didn't have it so easy. The Defendants only offered their prepared employees, who are deposed on a regular basis and knew what should be said and what shouldn't be. Lawyers fight to limit access to only those specially *prepped* employees. Additionally, I was disheartened to learn that every time we requested written responses, whether it was from the complaint or the interrogatories, their answers were purposefully composed, and allowed to be vague. Our answers, on the other hand, had to be replete with details and absolute answers to each and every question. At least, that's how I answered them. Here's an example of what I mean. Out of 267 responses on an Equifax Response—entitled

"Answer and Affirmative Defenses of Defendant Equifax Credit Information Services, Inc"—all but a handful of questions that we asked of them, were purposely vague and answered as follows: *"Equifax lacks knowledge or information sufficient to form a belief as to the truth of the allegation and therefore denies them."* Out of 267 responses, almost all were answered as if scripted and parroted to match any complaint against them. Another standard response was *"Equifax denies the allegations of paragraph 190."*

As you can see, not much information can be gleaned from their deliberately exceedingly vague responses. On the other hand, I responded to each question they ever requested of me with detail and honesty that was painstakingly time consuming.

I thought it must be a joke, yet, Alan said, "Answers to complaints and interrogatories are always answered that way. That's just the way it is."

"What?" I naively asked. "How could that be? What rule of law provides the reasoning behind the time and expense of requesting pertinent information when such answers, as the ones we received, are considered by the court as acceptable responses?

Over and over, the idea that the justice system is based on "equal justice for all" proved to be a myth. In reality, there can't possibly be equal justice with rules incorporated into the game that are designed to aid the unlimited funds of corporate Goliaths, ignoring the budget constraints that an average citizen must abide by.

Soon I was back in the car for another day of being deposed, certain to be filled with more questions that seemed unnecessary, more questions designed to wear me down emotionally and my attorneys down financially. On this particular day as I arrived at the deposition, the lawyers were all inside talking and I sat in the waiting room until Larry came out to me smiling.

"Fleet wants to make an offer to settle this morning," he said. "Only Fleet, they're breaking away from the other

Defendants." He handed me a piece of paper containing their written offer and after a lengthy discussion with Larry, the negotiations began.

I'm precluded from discussing any actual monetary negotiations we made that momentous day. I can say it was a very emotional day for me. I longed for my day in court and believed I could make a difference by creating a precedent if I could get my case in front of a jury. I learned that no matter how deeply you feel you've been wronged—getting in front of a jury is nowhere near as easily attainable as one might think. As much as I wanted to obtain that allusive case law, I was reminded on several occasions of the dreaded Rule 68. The words "Rule 68" were tossed around like a Frisbee by my husband and attorneys. "If a jury doesn't award you at least the amount of their offer, you <u>could</u> be responsible for their hefty corporate attorney fees and court costs from this date forward," I was strongly reminded.

Alan reassured me, "You can still have your day in court because the other defendants are not settled. All the details will have to come out. Plus, Fleet will have to testify because all along they have been assigning the blame to the credit bureaus."

After much discussion, we settled with Fleet that day in June 2000. I am prohibited to discuss the actual terms of the Agreement and amount settled on. I did however make sure that I would not be gagged (ever again) regarding the merits of the case, as I was in the first Agreement. I wasn't budging from that stance and they agreed noting the details of what transpired leading us to court had already been published and released in various on and off-line interviews. Equally as important, I wanted that initial "gag" Agreement that Shawmut drew up in 1994 nullified because they were the party that breached the Agreement. I wanted my voice back without fearing them.

After we reached a settlement, I also wanted one more, seemingly small thing. I asked Alan if I could get an apology I felt I deserved after nearly nine years of enduring their abusive actions. "I don't know, Denise, but I agree.

You certainly deserve one and, knowing how many people you have been interviewed by and how much media interest this case garnered, maybe they will give you one," he said. "Let me go talk to them, I'll be back." With that he walked away. Shortly, he came back with a statement written on paper and handed it to me. It read, *"Fleet regrets any difficulty suffered by the Richardsons in connection with this matter and reiterates its commitment to ensuring full compliance with all state and federal laws pertaining to consumer data reporting."*

"This is your apology. I told them that with the bad publicity they have been getting, it wouldn't hurt to say something nice. It's the best you're going to get for an apology and it's more than most consumers get."

I marveled at the different attitudes society has regarding criminal and civil cases. In a criminal case, if a defendant is found guilty and still claims his innocence he is frowned on by society for not being remorseful. However, the rules of remorse in a civil case often seem very different. When civil defendants lose - rarely—if ever—do they admit to any wrongdoing. In fact, just the opposite. They are quick to point out the fact that they admit to no wrongdoing and specifically deny any liability. It's sad because we teach our children (like our parents taught us) from a very young age to stand up and take responsibility for our actions. When we are wrong, admit it and take our comeuppance. Somehow it always appears that when a corporation is involved, they are no longer held to the same standard. They are not an individual—they are a corporation and it appears, with that title, you don't have to take ownership of any responsibility. That *is* the norm because corporations have a duty and responsibility to protect their shareholders...money.

Once we settled with Fleet, the remaining defendants continued with their depositions and soon, one by one, there were more requests to settle independently of each other. The next was Experian, which we settled with in September 2000. Then shortly after, we settled with Trans Union in December 2000.

Yet by that December, my life had already taken a major turn. My husband and I separated four months earlier, shortly after the Fleet Settlement. He retired from the Fire Department with his 30-year pension and his life revolved around him. He was rarely, if ever, home at night. It had grown apparent that during the years I was embroiled in the lawsuit, he had been left with too much time on his hands and we all know what they say about idle hands. His life hadn't been bombarded emotionally because, even though his credit reports were also riddled with errors, he never had to deal with any of it. In his one short deposition, he had spelled out the situation quite clearly. Over and over, when asked questions pertaining to a credit report or the particulars of the case, he said, "I don't know. Denise handled 99.9% of it." When asked a simple question like if he ever saw a particular form, his response was truthful. He said, "I may have. I don't know. She handled it all."

He was never deposed again—until our divorce. Prior to the divorce, I instructed Alan to split any funds we received equally with half sent to him and half to me. I was aware of how our relationship was affected by the stress of the lawsuit and other complications and I was trying to avoid any further battles. I just wanted an equal split of everything we acquired throughout our nearly 20 year marriage. Yet, nothing ever works out exactly as planned. In fact, the settlement with Trans Union was completed when the two of us were not even speaking and our Equifax settlement –well that took place *after* our divorce. Suffice to say that it was a very stressful time.

As the months moved forward so did the messy divorce. I finally got to the point where I just couldn't battle anymore and walked away from almost everything.

"You win. Keep it all—I just need to stop fighting. I don't want anymore battles. I can't take it! I *need* my life back!"

I soon moved to Florida. I fled the cold winters and the small town where we had lived. I chose sanity over money, and my small but comfortable home in Florida over the commodities acquired over the course of a 20-year marriage. Coming out of these major battles, I knew I needed distance to find a way to pull my overly stressed, emotionally torn, battered mind, health and life back together. The only thing I missed was my family and friends, but a new, peaceful life was on the horizon. My friends all knew what I was up against and knew my leaving would be the best avenue I could take to a better life. Even Alan who had come to know the details and reasons for my pending divorce said, "You must be crazy to stay here. If you have a chance to get away, go to Florida—go!"

In the end, I was well aware of the steep price I paid by simply paying my mortgage without tracking my payments. Prolonged stress and enormous frustrations can take their toll on your health and every facet in your life. Don't do what I did and try to fight the battle on your own. I let too many years go by thinking they would make good on their promises to correct their errors. Hindsight being 20/20, I could have saved many years of aggravations and myself a lot of pain had I known my rights and turned to legal representation after their first broken promise-instead of waiting years.

Chapter Lesson: Hit them where it hurts—in their pocketbooks

Sadly, the law is often not as obvious and simple as consumers wish it to be. Laws arc intended to protect us but, all too often, they are riddled with loopholes that can be used against us by experienced corporate attorneys trying to slip their clients out of any responsibility for their actions. Nonetheless, the courts are the only tool consumers have to utilize consumer protections laws entitling them to stop and prevent abuses. Of course, like everything else in life, damages are measured in dollars and finances instead of the victim's frustrations and headaches. Even so, these damages are very important, especially when a court decides to award punitive damages. These are meted out if it is proven that the defendant's actions were malicious or outrageous. It's not always easy, and quite often an uphill battle (when it shouldn't be) to obtain a ruling allowing the collection of punitive damages. First, the plaintiff must prove the corporation's conduct was outrageous and no person should have to endure what their actions or inactions caused. It must also be proved that the defendant knowingly or with malicious intent caused that damage to the plaintiff. It may sound easy but the courts don't always see it from the consumer's point of view.

Punitive damages, however, are one of the most important aspects of a consumer court decision because they hold the abusing corporation liable with damage amounts based on their net worth, not on the plaintiff's actual loss. Punitive actions make the defendant's stakes higher and therefore carry more weight than a slap on the wrist. They are meant to both punish the offender as well as deter them from repeating their offenses against another innocent party. There have been cases where it appears to the average citizen that multi-million dollar figures awarded to damaged victims were much too high. Yet, all too often, these mega corporations don't stop their abuses or take the required steps to stop it from happening to others until it hits them in the pocket book.

Let me offer an example of how punitive damages can be powerful weapons *against* greed. Let's pretend that companies who manufacture toys, automobiles, or household products are only held liable for damages at a flat rate of say $250,000. These same companies could easily find it to be cheaper to cut corners with safety, leaving substandard products on the market, and take their chances on being sued, than it would be to simply create better products in the first place. It is very possible that it makes more financial sense to take the gamble knowing that few people will actually file suit and fewer still will win. What would deter them from taking this stance? The deterrent in place now is the open threat of a lawsuit wherein they risk being held liable for punitive damages. Also, the likelihood of a large court settlement makes it easier for a consumer to find an attorney willing to take on a Goliath corporation.

I am not at all advocating suing someone for the sake of suing them. Any truly innocent party that has ever been caught up in the justice system never makes a decision to go through those doors lightly. However, we must fight to keep our courtroom doors open and continue to fight for a system of equality.

Consumer protection laws that hold corporations accountable for negligence, fraud and cutting corners on safety need to be strong and void of loopholes to ensure corporations don't place profits above safety.

Chapter 10 – *What Lies in the Past*

We'll look into it...
Don't worry...
We'll research the matter and get back to you...

When most people hear those phrases they feel a sense of relief knowing the words are intended to comfort and reassure them that there is no need to worry and all will be okay. In my life, however, when I hear the same phrases the picture my mind conjures up is one of big red flags waving and internal voices screaming DANGER AHEAD as lights blink brightly on and off.

I don't think anyone truly knew to what extent these words both seemed, and in actuality had, the opposite effect on me. What nobody knew was I had endured other damaging domino-like events in the past that had remained buried away inside me and hearing those words "don't worry" brought everything back to the forefront. I couldn't help but take a look back to the 1970s, when another series of inter-locking events far out of the realm of my control occurred. Perhaps these domino-like events will shed additional light as to why their broken promises struck me with such force.

I was twenty-three and I had a two-and-a-half-year old daughter to support. I had married and divorced my childhood sweetheart and was still living in Vermont. We married young and also became parents young, at the age of only 21. Even though my childhood sweetheart and I had been together for several years, it became obvious we married too early in our young lives. After the brief marriage, I found myself on my own for the fist time in my young life but managed to get an apartment, daycare for my daughter and a job nearby. I bought a used car. It was a red 1976 Toyota Celica that I fell in love with because it symbolized my freedom and the first asset I could claim solely as mine. I was living paycheck to paycheck while working in the office of a manufacturing plant where I was beginning to enjoy my new life, my job and my co-workers. Then one unsuspecting day, out of the blue, we were told that our plant was closing its doors. Though a few people would be asked to transfer to the Keene, New Hampshire plant, we were all potentially in jeopardy of losing our jobs.

Keene was located about twenty miles away, over large mountainous terrain that I was not excited about traveling over each day. I was especially leery of the drive during the harsh New England winters that grew dark at four in the afternoon. When dealing with the black ice, heavy snow, and ice storms that occurred on a regular basis, traveling this road could be treacherous. The commute would also mean that I would often be dropping my daughter off at daycare in the early morning darkness and picking her up in the darkness of evening. It makes for a very bleak and sometimes scary ride. The transfer also meant more money diverted to additional hours of daycare for Jadie. All of those issues aside, I needed the job. Eventually, my employer offered me the position of Secretary to the Director of Inventory which came with better perks and a salary increase to boot.

"Wow!" I thought. "Let's celebrate." My friend Linda and I headed out that night in my much loved and *paid for* 1976 red Toyota Celica. We hadn't a care in the world as we cranked up Billy Joel's cassette in the car, singing every word out loud as we traveled Main Street looking for our friends. Within just a few short minutes we were at Mort's, our local meeting spot, a place where many of us met up on weekends to find out what everyone's plan for the night was. It was that fateful Friday evening when Keith sauntered in and pointed to the parking lot where he had just parked his bright new shiny yellow Camero. Impressed, we all asked him if we could take it for a ride. Surprisingly, he not only said yes but nonchalantly suggested we switch cars for the night. It was never clear what possessed him to make the offer, but it was a temptation that I couldn't resist.

Before accepting his exciting proposition, I relayed my fears. "What if I get in an accident with your car? What if someone dings the door or it breaks down while I have it?"

Keith squelched my fears, as if I was needlessly worrying about something that could never possibly happen, by stating, "Don't worry; nothing will happen. The same risk is on my hands by taking your car—don't worry."

"But," I thought, "his car is brand new, my car isn't." He didn't have such a high risk—or so it seemed. Nonetheless, Keith and I eventually agreed to switch cars and exchanged car keys. I didn't take the Camero very far. My friends and I drove it to a couple of other local hangouts and around the Main Street drag a few times. Friday nights traveling Main Street meant yelling out to friends, showing off our vehicles or catching up with what everyone was doing. We thought it was fun to drive this hot looking Camero, turning heads and enjoying the night. Our fears were replaced with just feeling cool—riding along in a bright yellow muscle car. We were very careful, driving only a few short circles through town and then home, where the car was parked safely in my driveway.

If I had only known that making that decision would be the push that sent me off the pecuniary cliff and force Keith directly into one. It turned out to be a decision from which the inter-locking consequences of that momentous night would haunt me for years to come.

Unfortunately, Keith's voyage in my car was not as uneventful as my journey in his. I awoke to a loud knock at the door. I looked at the clock—it was 3:00 a.m. As I peeked out the window, I saw a police cruiser in my driveway and a policeman waiting at the door. My heart started to pound and in those few seconds I thought of every imaginable possibility as to what brought him to my doorstep –except the real reason he was there.

"Are you the owner of a 1976 red Toyota Celica"?

"I am," I replied, growing more suspicious by the moment.

"I'm sorry to tell you that it has been totaled in an accident tonight."

My heart stopped. He went on to tell me "the driver lost control of the car less than a couple of miles from here on Sunset Road."

Sunset is a twisting, turning, typical Vermont back road with a speed limit of 25 mph—for good reason.

"He was going at least three times the speed limit when he lost control and hit a large stone ledge." The officer continued the bad news, "He hit with such force that I would be surprised if you hadn't heard the explosion from here."

I never imagined I would be driving the yellow Camero to the hospital just hours after exchanging keys. Keith was in critical condition, in a coma. Apparently, the only thing that saved his life was the fact that his window was open, which ejected him from the car as it rolled over. Thank God he was alive –I just prayed he would be strong enough to make a full recovery.

When he woke the doctors upgraded his prognosis to stable. He was seriously hurt and had months, if not years, of rehabilitation ahead of him. His immediate recovery required him to remain in the hospital for weeks to follow. Finally, with knowledge that Keith would completely recover, I was soon able to realize what our exchanging keys that night really resulted in—I had no car and no way of getting to work in Keene. I borrowed Keith's car to travel to and from work, the hospital and Jadie's daycare but the truth was he couldn't afford to keep his car on the road for too long without being able to work.

I couldn't help but think of how important it was going to be for me to get a stable car for commuting each day. I couldn't take the chance of a breakdown on that horrible mountainous road in the winter and miss picking up Jadie at daycare. Soon after starting my new job, I eventually received enough money from insurance proceeds for a down payment on a new car. It would be my first *new* car. I felt naively safe in being able to handle the car payments because my salary had increased with this new position. I was also entitled to raises, based on my job performance and reviews would occur every six months, or so I was told. This was a well-established business that had no intentions of closing its doors so odds were good I would be there quite a while.

As an Executive Secretary, it was my duty each morning to cross the threshold from my desk to my boss' office to take dictation as well as discuss various other duties my position called for. I picked up the duties of this position quite quickly and realized it was not going to be a difficult job. Knowing this, I figured that I might actually enjoy the drive. I could consider it valuable time to unwind while traveling from work before the rush of duties involved in being a single mom.

My boss appeared to be at least 20 years my senior. I'm not sure exactly how many years, because at that age I perceived anyone not in their twenties to be old. He had grey hair, weighed probably 250 pounds and his personality seemed to express that he thought very highly of himself. He often spoke inappropriately about his home life and after-hours activities. I was subjected to constant sexual innuendos and continual incidental touching. I did what I could to avoid too much personal contact but, as his secretary, it was often very difficult.

I settled into the routine of the job. As I imagined, it was not difficult work. Eventually, my boss discovered that my birthday was only a month away. He kept insisting, "I'm taking you out to lunch for your birthday. Plan on it." He repeated this demand on several occasions. I couldn't understand why he was making it a big deal but tried to reassure myself that he was merely trying to make a nice gesture and show me he was happy with my work. My birthday arrived and by then I had grown increasingly uncomfortable with the constant innuendos about his sex life. The morning dictation had grown awkward as he would often interrupt work to ask inappropriate questions about my personal life and attempted to gain information on my sex life. Being in my early 20s and having a man old enough to be my father delving unprofessionally into my personal life not only made me feel uncomfortable—it honestly grossed me out. He made it clear he was flirting with me. He would often rub up against my leg while handing me papers, walk up behind me to rub my shoulders or run his fingers through my long hair.

In the 1970s, there was no discussion of sexual harassment in the work place—none. We lived in a very different world back then. I certainly didn't know of any possible rights I had to combat his constant harassment. If there were rights available to me back then, I was too young and naive to know of them. Then my birthday came along with the specter of this dreaded, so-called lunch date. I tried making excuses. I claimed that I was too busy to go to lunch and that we should just order in. He refused and became insistent.

"We agreed to this a month ago," he said. "I am not taking 'no' for an answer."

As we walked out of the office together, he informed the receptionist that we would be back in an hour. I nervously climbed into his car and stared out the window as he drove. I silently hoped for any sign of escape from this lunch. As we rolled along, he suddenly pulled his car into a fast food restaurant and I thought, "Great, we're here, close to work. It won't be that bad." Then, I watched in horror as he drove up to the drive-thru and asked me what I wanted.

"Why are you at the drive thru?" I asked, fearing what his answer might be.

"It's such a beautiful day," he replied with a wide grin on his face. "Let's go eat in the park to get some sunshine."

How was I going to make it through this hour?

He pulled his car into a secluded area of the park and turned the engine off. I felt stiff and on guard as I sat there, leaning into the front passenger side door. My body language screamed, "Back off." Suddenly, he leaned over to my side of the car. I was on guard. It appeared that as he was leaning in to kiss me. I held my breath and prepared for the worst. He reached down by my legs and felt for something on the floor under my seat. He pulled out a small box and a card. Relief came over me and I apprehensively opened the card. He had hand written a little poetic verse on how attracted he was to me and signed it, "Love, Dean." I immediately felt a sense of dread come over me but acted cool, as if I didn't understand what he was alluding to. I was young and really didn't know how to deal with his advances.

I nervously laughed while opening the red package that had a dazzling, heart-covered bow on it. It was a bottle of perfume. I knew I had to stay on guard and get him to drive us back to work. I told him I did not feel well. "We'd better get back to the office, I really need to use a bathroom," I said, trying to sound less nervous than I was.

He started the car with a pout on his face as if I had snatched away his toy. He drove back to work with intentional sloth, moving at a speed which seemed to be about five miles an hour. When we finally returned to the office, I immediately bolted for the ladies room. I sat there wondering how I was going to continue working like this. I kept myself busy in the plant that day away from my desk. The rest of the afternoon seemed to drag on for many more hours than actually passed. Before I left, I went into his office to let him know that I didn't think his card was appropriate. But much to my dismay, he just smiled as if I hadn't said a word. I didn't know what to make of his reaction. Then I quickly turned, walked out of the office, grabbed my purse and left.

I was up all night dwelling on how I was going to handle this—and how much I needed this job. The next day I called in sick. I just couldn't face him. I had no idea what to do, but needed time to think about how to handle the situation he created in my life. About ten in the morning my doorbell rang. I felt a piercing stab in my gut as I peered out the window. I couldn't believe my eyes. There he stood, as big as life on my front door step. My home was over twenty miles away, in another state. I didn't have any idea how he knew where I lived. I opened the door slightly and immediately became defensive. "What are you doing here?" were the words that rolled off my tongue.

"I just wanted to check on you and make sure you were okay," he said, smiling as he spoke. He went on to tell me he just happened to be in Vermont on business. He had flowers and a card in his hands. Almost immediately, he lunged forward, pushing the door open and put his arms around me in a bear hug. My reaction was to push him away as hard as I could. A sense of panic flooded over me.

"I brought you flowers to make you feel better," he said as he handed the offerings to me. He placed the card and flowers on my kitchen table and stood there as if waiting for something.

"Dean, I'm really sick and I'm sorry but you really need to leave," I said. These seemed to be the only words I could get out of my mouth despite the many thoughts rushing through my head—fearful thoughts both of him and of losing my job.

After he left I sat at a kitchen chair and cried as I stared at the flowers he left. I opened the envelope to find a get-well card with an underlined inscription reading, "Love, Dean."

I can't help but reflect that if those events were to transpire today, what happened in that office would have been handled in quite a different way than it was; but back then, nobody discussed sexual harassment on the job or even knew there was a name for it. If there were laws against it then, I certainly didn't know of them. Even though I was 23, very naïve and hadn't heard of any sexual harassment laws, I knew his actions were not at all acceptable or normal behavior for an employer many years my senior-but at 23, I was a far cry from understanding the ramifications of speaking out –and really had no clue how to handle it. After many hours of crying and pondering how desperately I needed to keep my paychecks coming in, I decided I would take the cards, the present and the flowers into work with me the next day and bring it all to the attention of Dean's boss, Mr. Mullins, the President of the corporation. I naively believed he would help me fix this. Mr. Mullins was always nice to me and seemed to recognize I was a valuable employee. He had, on several occasions, told me what a great job I was doing.

I gathered up all the courage I could muster to head to work that morning. I planned on meeting with Mr. Mullins the first chance he gave me. I buzzed his office as soon as I arrived at work. "Mr. Mullins, I was wondering if you could give me a few minutes of your time," I asked nervously. "I have something very important I need to talk to you about."

There was no pause. He immediately responded, "Of course, Denise, come right in now."

I grabbed my valuable paper bag, filled with the incriminating evidence. It carried all my hopes that they would see my desperate and legitimate need for help. I walked into his big corner office and saw Ken, the comptroller of the company, was in the office as well, seated at the conference table to the right of Mr. Mullins. Armed only with that bag containing the cards and gifts from Dean, I nervously sat at the conference table. I pulled out each item, informing both of them about the sickening chain of events that left me feeling so distressed that I had called in sick the day before. I explained to them what happened each morning while taking dictation, the details of my birthday lunch and why this man's appearance at my home was so unsettling to me.

"Perhaps you could speak to him for me?"

As I was telling my story, speaking through tears of fear, I saw each of them reading over the cards, passing them back and forth while smirking at each other.

"We'll look into this matter, Denise. We can see this has upset you. Why don't you go home today and take a day or two off while we decide how to handle this with Dean."

"Don't worry," added Ken. "Go home and relax a couple of days while we look into it."

I got up from the table, knees visibly shaking, thanked them and walked out of the office. So young and naive then, I kept wondering—*would they "fix things" so we could work together? Could we place all of this in the past – move on and start anew?* I nervously contemplated what could be happening back in those offices, and what was being said to Dean. I decided to look at the situation optimistically. After all, they had told me not to worry. *Don't worry, worry, worry . . .*

I couldn't have been more wrong. The next day early in the morning, there came another knock at my door. This time it was Ken, the comptroller. He looked rather glum and did not look up at me when I answered the door. He said, "We need to talk." He took a few steps in and reached for a chair at the kitchen table. As he seated himself, he continued, "Denise, we feel in light of the recent events that took place, it would be too difficult for you to work for Dean anymore. Furthermore, it would be too difficult for you to work in the same building as him." He looked at his shoes, and not me.

"What does that mean, Ken? I don't understand," I said.

"We wish you well, Denise, and this is very difficult for us, but we are letting you go."

I stood there in shock, unable to pull any words together in my mouth. He handed me an envelope—it had two weeks' pay in it.

"I'm sorry Denise, but we will give you an excellent reference," Ken offered before walking out the door.

My world came crashing down around me. I don't even remember if I said goodbye to him. I just remember the mixture of shock, betrayal and disillusionment I felt.

Two weeks' pay doesn't cut it when you live paycheck to paycheck, with a two-year old to support, new car payments, rent and daycare all needing to be paid. I sat in a chair, just staring out the window with tears rolling down my face for hours. *What was I going to do? How would I pay my rent and make my car payments?* A car I had just recently bought to travel safely to my new job.

I had to find a job, and find it fast. I needed to contact my bank and see if they would work with me on my car payments. *Was there a way I could pay less for a month or so and make it up in the future? I would give them what I could until I had a regular paycheck again, but would they work with me until then?* I couldn't save any money by taking Jadie out of daycare because they required a full prior month's notice or I would be charged anyway. I had already stretched my paycheck to get by too many times. Questions about what to do continued running through my head, like when the last song you hear on the radio gets stuck on replay. I contacted my bank, the lien holder of my car. I let them know that I didn't have the money to make my full payment on time that month. I explained that I had lost my job and would soon find a new one.

"When my paychecks start coming in regularly, I can catch up quickly— would you be willing to work with me in the interim, maybe allow me to make interest only payments for a couple of months?

The bank representative sounded understanding, "Don't worry, I've looked into it. It will be okay." She understood my concerns and assured me, "Just send in what you feel you can afford as a sort of 'good faith' payment. When your finances return to normal, you can send in more and catch up within a few months."

She seemed very matter-of-fact about the matter, as if mine was a normal situation and the solution was a routine procedure.

What a relief! This conversation calmed a lot of my stress. I felt a huge sense of relief fill the air. It might be tight for a while but we, Jadie and I, would get through it. *Everything happens for a reason.* I always believed in that adage –from a very young age. After all, no more traveling to Keene would mean saving an hour a day. All would be alright, eventually. I looked over my budget as best I could and scavenged twenty dollars for the "good faith" car payment. I wrote out the check and mailed it in.

A few weeks later, I started my new job, a position that I found by calling companies listed in the yellow pages. "Are you doing any clerical hiring?" I would ask. I would repeat that question at least twenty times before I heard the response, "Yes, can you come in for an interview today?"

I found a job at a local manufacturing plant and worked in the business office performing data entry. I was fairly happy with the position. Always the optimist, I believed that after a few paychecks I would be back on track. Shortly after noon, I left for lunch. I walked to the parking lot expecting to find my car. As anyone who has forgotten where they parked can testify, panic sets in immediately upon discovering that your car isn't where you thought you left it. *Did I lock the doors? I was on a hill—did I place it in park when I got out? Do I even have the keys with me?* As these questions ran through my head it dawned on me that my car might not have been stolen. I thought about my two partial bank payments and what the representative had told me on the phone. It hit me with such fear that I froze. *Could the bank have taken my car?*

I ran back inside and called the bank. Now instead of dreading that my car had been stolen, I was hoping that theft was the case—I had insurance for that. I got on the phone and very quickly received the news that the car was no longer "mine."

In a state of fear and panic, I had the presence of mind to turn to a good friend. David was a friend I grew up with and we remained close friends. David said he would come and get me and take me to the bank. I told my boss that I needed to leave for the rest of the day. I don't remember if I even gave him a reason though I'm sure he saw the state of mind I was in. David showed up and together we drove to the bank. I walked in expecting only to make use of David as moral support as I explained about my good faith payments. Almost immediately, David piped in with his own agenda. "How much does she owe to bring her up to date?"

I was stunned. The loan officer hit a few keys on his computer and scowled "the entire loan balance and all late fees would need to be paid in full."

"I can't pay that much," David volunteered. "But I can certainly pay enough to get her back on track." I was surprised and impressed by this gesture. I knew that the bank couldn't turn down such a benevolent offer. David was a true friend and gentleman.

Unfortunately, the banks of this enlightened day and age are not bound by rules of chivalry and David's intervention was nixed by the bank representative immediately. "I'm sorry," he said. "Once a car is repossessed—the loan is called in—it must be paid in full."

I'm sure I mumbled, screamed or cried something about the nice woman on the phone who told me it would be fine if I made "good faith" payments of what I could afford. I didn't know her name or the name of the supervisor she had "looked into it" with. I made the man look up my smaller payments. I knew it had to mean something—at least show my effort and good faith. Despite my desperation, nothing worked. The only thing we had in writing was the original loan papers and those gave the bank every right to take my car.

I left the bank without my car and found myself back in my apartment sitting at the table with tears streaming down my cheeks as I realized the unmistakable reality that I was again –without a car.

Every action has a reaction but how good or how bad often depends on how many dominos fall.

We'll look into it . . .

Don't worry, worry, worry . . .

All those years later, hearing Shawmut and Fleet representatives repeat those same words, the same sense of fear and powerlessness came over me. It proved to me again that such platitudes were synonymous with trouble, with a capital "T." Over the course of my life, I found I had legitimate reasons to become suspicious and alarmed when hearing what most people would find to be simple, innocuous phrases. I was no longer a single mother of 23, but this ancient chain of events, over two decades ago came flooding back with obvious and striking similarities. The fact is, like the rest of humanity, events transpire that we have no control of and carry with them great consequences. They interlock with each other and often alter who we are; changing us into advocates or activists who *must* fight for change.

Chapter Lesson: Every Action Has a Reaction

Like ghosts from the past, consumers can be haunted by their credit mistakes or errors. In order to be a responsible consumer, you must be aware of every area in which your credit can be affected. Be aware of the following, often dangerous situations:

- Blindly sending in payments, whether on an auto loan, student loan, or a mortgage. Always verify how each and every penny is being applied. If you don't get a monthly statement or can't access your account online, call them every month and ask for a payment history schedule.

- Accounts that you pay into or draw money out of that give you no access to a real person. You should always be able to contact a real person, preferably by phone or in person, in case you find yourself in the worst case scenario. Computers can only give so much advice!

- Closing accounts you don't use is not always the best advice and shouldn't be done without the guidance of someone well versed in the effects of credit scoring and reporting. Closing accounts can result in a balance/limit ratio which could actually damage your score because you appear to be using all of your available credit. Many consumers that have excellent credit scores above 720 (out of a possible 850) have access to a high balance of untouched available credit.

- Do not rely on the credit monitoring systems that the credit bureaus and credit card companies offer. Oftentimes they will only monitor the data reported to one credit bureau-not all three. Additionally – having had a protection plan in place at the time of my nightmare battles –I was never notified when the erroneous and derogatory information was placed on my file. Not once was I notified by them of negative information inserted into my credit file—I had to find out myself through my own monitoring or of course, being humiliated with a credit denial which soon proved to me their monitoring system was as inadequate as their reporting system!

- Utilize the many consumer friendly advocate sites and consumer communities on the web. I list many in this book. Consumer Advocates have spent their lives fighting to protect our rights— it's time we unite our voices. The web is an excellent means to that end. Together, it just might be possible to make a real difference.

For more information, on credit scoring and the credit system, an excellent resource is Evan Hendricks' book entitled *Credit Scores and Credit Reports: How the system really works and what you can do*, which is widely available in its second edition.

Chapter 11 – _Moving Forward-_
Looking Back

In September 2000, I made the move to Florida and lived on the beach for a couple of months before looking for a new home—and the responsibilities that came with it. Living on the beach gave me a sense of being on vacation and allowed me some tranquility that I desperately needed. In December, after numerous negotiations, we agreed to settle and end the case against Trans Union. No sooner did we settle when along came a frightening and eerie brand new experience. I was about to find out I had recently become a victim of the traditional type of identity theft—where a thief steals your credit card information and pretends to be you.

I found out about it while shopping one Sunday afternoon when paying for a purchase with my Platinum MBNA credit card. The cashier rang up my purchases and suddenly looked up at me as she was reading from the screen of her cash register.

"The credit card company wants to talk to you, Ms. Richardson," she said. "I am going to have to give them a call."

"Well, okay but why?" I asked as I turned to look at the line forming behind me. I ran through the credit card's history in my mind. I had a zero balance on this card and I had not been making any unusual purchases. There is no reason this charge shouldn't go through, I assured myself.

The cashier picked up the phone then after a few moments, her eye turned to me, "They want to speak with you." As soon as I put my ear to the phone, I promptly told my credit card company rep that I didn't understand the reason for this embarrassing hold up.

"Ms. Richardson," he responded. "We're very sorry but we have been trying to reach you. We think you have become a victim of identity theft. Did you recently purchase a series of one-way or round-trip airline tickets from Rome or Swiss Air totaling over $9,000.00?"

My heart began to race and I quickly replied, "Oh my God, NO! I haven't purchased any airline tickets!"

"That's what we thought," he said. "Give the phone back to the cashier and we will let her put this charge through. When you get home please call us back and speak with the Fraud Department. We can discuss this further and get it straightened out."

I couldn't help but be alarmed and feared what might be on the horizon. How were they able to get my credit card information? What else would these thieves steal? I had the card—there it was safely in my wallet—but they obviously had enough information to purchase airline tickets.

As soon as I arrived home, I immediately contacted the fraud department. What I learned shocked me. Originally, someone at Swiss Air was suspicious of the purchases and contacted my credit card company who then also became suspicious and agreed with the airline that the purchases appeared to be an attempted identity theft. They immediately declined payment for the airline tickets. "However, the representative relayed with amazement, additional charges were allowed to be charged to your card after that initial denial and totaled over $9,000.00. All of the charges were made from outside the country, apparently from Rome."

The good news was the credit card company immediately released me from any liability for the illegal charges and asked me for my cooperation in prosecuting the individuals –if they were able to apprehend them. They further relayed there was one American name listed on the charged tickets and they were going to try to trace the theft through that person. Of course, I offered to cooperate and help in holding the thieves responsible.

That was the end of my conversation with the fraud department but not the end of my worries. A few weeks later I received my credit card statement. As I reviewed it, I saw

141

all the names of the intended passengers and the illegal charges applied to my credit card balance. I contacted the fraud department immediately and their rep explained that the reversal of charges simply hadn't caught up with my account by the statement closing date. The credit, they assured me, would be applied and reflected on my next month's statement. They advised me to only pay the charges I was responsible for— that one particular Sunday purchase made on the date they had alerted me to the problem.

I did so immediately and soon happily found that they kept their promise. The next month, the credit for the $9,000.00+ was applied and the incident was never reported to the credit bureaus. How nice, I thought, that I would not have to think of this again. That is, until nine months later when 9/11 came along.

I finally found a townhouse that I fell in love with, bought it and moved in June 2001. The divorce battle caused additional stress, more attorneys, court filings and depositions, and was much more intense than I ever thought it would be—or had to be. Alan and I continued to build our case against the remaining defendant (Equifax) through emails and constant telephone conversations. Things were anything but peaceful. After the morning of September 11th, however, the time directly before would seem almost idyllic. Like the rest of the world, 9/11 jolted my life into perspective. I clearly saw my problems were nothing compared with the horrors that ripped apart our hearts that unforgettable morning. We all remember those following days as we were glued to the developing news listening intently to news anchors and journalists advising us to contact the FBI if we saw *anything* that didn't look right or *anything* out of the ordinary. There was a constant scroll that ran on the bottom of the TV screen imploring all of us citizens to report *any* suspicious activity we may have seen during or prior to that painful day.

I was lying in bed one night watching the 11 o'clock news and listened intently as the anchor again relayed the FBI's call for information, no matter how minor it may seem to us. Something struck me –I sprang up into a sitting position holding my hands on my face. I began to remember the fraudulently purchased airline tickets from Rome. They were purchased just ten or so months before 9/11. There had been a total of 10 tickets purchased—three one-way and seven round-trip tickets. The passenger names were not of American dissent, were foreign and not easily pronounceable. The destination cities were all around the Middle East and Europe. The airline codes appeared to indicate travel to Milan, Italy, Amsterdam, Netherlands, and Dubai in the United Arab Emirates, purchased with "Italian Lira" –at least, that's what the statement indicated.

I couldn't help but fear there could be a connection. I knew I needed to contact the FBI's 800 number and, at least, report the information. Let them decide if it was pertinent or not, I thought. Was there a connection between the illegally purchased airline tickets and terrorism? Was it significant that I was living in the same city where Mohammed Atta and others resided before that fateful, horrific day?

I contacted the FBI the next morning. When an agent came on the line, I told him that I didn't know if what I was about to tell him was pertinent to their investigation or not. However, I wanted to report what happened to my credit card months earlier. I informed him that a total of $9,000.00 worth of airline tickets were fraudulently purchased by *someone* using my credit card information from outside the United States.

He was silent for a moment and then asked me if he could place me on hold telling me he was transferring me to an agent and asked me to supply him with all the pertinent information. A couple of minutes passed and another agent picked up the line and I explained all I was privy too. As I listed every name on my credit card statement, which of course I had held on to like everything else I received from creditors, the agent took it down letter for letter, every airline code and every digit on the statement including, of course, the passenger names (which I spelled out) and my account number. I asked him if it would be helpful if I faxed him the statement.

"There's really no need to. I'm going to call your credit card company to follow up on this and will obtain the statement and further information from them directly."

I also informed the FBI of the only two places I had used that particular credit card just prior to the theft. I used it once while shopping in the Keys over Thanksgiving in 2000 and once when I purchased furniture at a local furniture store. I never heard another word about that eerie identity theft, but to this date, it still lingers in my mind. I often wonder how those thieves obtained my account information and if there was any horrible connection to the events of 9/11. Also, this incident proved to me how identity theft and credit issues threaten more than just a consumer's wallet and bank account. Physical danger and national security issues could also be at stake.

Meanwhile in my legal battle, my case against Equifax had taken a turn. Equifax filed a "*Motion for Summary Judgment*"—a common, formal request to the judge, asking him to release them from any responsibility for their actions and to have the case against them dismissed. This was their way of being free from any culpability, which I believed was their strategy all along. Knowing the law states that a plaintiff cannot be paid more than once for the same damages, their twist was: "Hey, she's already been paid for damages by the other defendants, so let us off the hook, judge. We didn't do anything wrong." Equifax's attorney had adopted an attitude and posture that seemed to show his dislike for me had grown personal. Though it may have been all my perception, the remarks he continued to make to my attorney about me surprised even Alan, who came to share my opinion. The judge made his decision and, thankfully, didn't see it <u>all</u> their way.

He ruled in favor of Equifax as to intentional infliction of emotional distress (which meant that punitive damages were disallowed), but he didn't let the case against Equifax be totally dismissed. This paved the way for a trial dealing with actual damages and not punitive ones, a trial that would never come to be. Equifax seemed to gloat in their next correspondence to us because their liability and the threat of a "big money" settlement dissipated with the ruling against punitive damages. Punitive damages and case law was all they feared. That's what deters corporations from actions of abuse and provides the incentive to stop them from playing games with consumers' lives. If I continued to seek a precedent as case law and Rule 68 came into play, or the judge reduced any award from the jury based on what I was already paid, I could end up paying for their fees, a hypothesis of which they never failed to remind me. It was a game of chess that was played by the defendants' attorneys expertly, proving they certainly had the necessary experience and game strategy.

On the other hand, the part of the ruling that determined whether or not there was a question of material fact, which would allow this case to be determined by a jury of my peers, was decided in my favor. The judge ruled that we could move to court. Finally, I thought, a jury could now decide if Equifax had the mandated "*reasonable procedures*" in place to stop it from happening to others.

Along with the judge's ruling though, came pressure from every direction to settle –now more than ever. Finally, in November 2001, more than a year after moving to Florida and one month shy of a full decade being embroiled in battles within the banking and credit industries –it was all about to end. I had no idea that as the courtroom doors closed and my battles *appeared* to be over, a new set of events were brewing on the horizon –events that would lead to this project's birth –causing this story to be told.

Chapter Lesson: The Judge's Decision

The judge handed down a decision in the case, which brought about both the end of the case –and even more hard learned lessons. The decision was lengthy and loaded with complex legal jargon which is difficult for the layman to understand. I have broken down the pertinent parts of his decision here.

1. Equifax filed a "Motion for Summary Judgment."

A Motion for a Summary Judgment is a request for the judge to make a pre-trial ruling that would essentially release Equifax from the case and release them from liability. To put it bluntly, they were claiming that I didn't have a case against them.

According to the law, Equifax could be entitled to (win) summary judgment "if the pleading, depositions, answers to interrogatories, and admissions on file, together with the affidavits, if any, show that there is no genuine issue as to any material fact and that the moving party (Equifax) is entitled to a judgment as a matter of law." Fed. R. Civ. P. 56(c).

Summary judgment involves shifting burdens of proof between the defendant and the plaintiff. Initially the burden of proof falls on the defendant but quickly shifts to the plaintiff who must provide the necessary evidence proving the issues in question are "genuine trial worthy issues." When the judge rules on a party's summary judgment motion (in this case, Equifax), he must review the evidence in the light most favorable to the nonmoving party (me) and draw all *reasonable inferences* in *that* party's favor.

In order to survive a Summary Judgment motion the plaintiff must present confirmatory evidence to rebut each of the defendant's claims, or *vice versa*. Additionally, the evidence must illustrate that the facts can't be speculative or problematic—they must have substance in that they clearly depict two differing versions of the truth which a fact finder (jury) must resolve. So, in order to successfully defeat Equifax's motion for summary judgment, we had to present evidence to show the judge that we had a case, and that case was strong enough to warrant the intervention of a jury.

CRAs often petition for summary judgment when they are brought to court by consumers. In fact, the CRAs' motions are frequently boiler plate, merely templates of what they have used in other cases with the names changed in all the right places. In my opinion, their actions and their boiler plate answers speak volumes to the countless consumer initiated cases against them...their system isn't working.

2. Equifax <u>DID</u> violate provisions of the FCRA

In order to present my case against Equifax to the jury, we first had to survive their Motion for Summary Judgment which meant we had to provide evidence to the judge, supporting the assertions in our original complaint, and to rebut their claims and prove ours. Here is a breakdown of the most pertinent parts of the judge's findings. The entirety of the judge's Decision can be found online.

- **Reasonable procedures**:

Under the FCRA, a consumer reporting agency must follow "reasonable procedures to assure maximum possible accuracy" regarding the information contained in a consumer's credit report. A claim of noncompliance . . . consists of four elements: (1) inaccurate information was included in a consumer's credit report; (2) the inaccuracy was due to defendant's failure to follow reasonable procedures to assure maximum possible accuracy; (3) the consumer suffered injury; and (4) the consumer's injury was caused by the inclusion of the inaccurate entry."

Equifax argued among other things that they relied on Fleet and Shawmut to send them accurate information. The judge's decision, however, concluded, "The Court declines to say that relying on creditors for accurate credit information constitutes a reasonable procedure as a matter of law where, as here, the credit reporting agency had reason to know of the dispute between the plaintiffs and Equifax."

- **Reasonable investigation of disputes:**

The FCRA provides, in part, that when a consumer notifies a credit reporting agency that information contained in his or her report may be inaccurate, "the agency shall reinvestigate free of charge and record the current status of the disputed information, or delete the item from the file."

Equifax argued that the statute requires a credit reporting agency only to confirm the accuracy of the information with the original source of information but imposes no mandate on the agency to take additional steps to confirm the accuracy of the disputed information.

The judge's decision pointed out that "...*the majority of courts hold that a credit reporting agency must, in certain circumstances, verify the accuracy of its initial source of information. The judge continued, "...Moreover, the courts have determined in this context that 'whether a reasonable investigation has been conducted is generally a question for the jury.' Viewing the record in the light most favorable to the plaintiffs, the Court concludes that the plaintiffs' section 1681i claim survives Equifax's motion for summary judgment.*"

3. Equifax <u>DID</u> have a responsibility towards damages:

Equifax also challenged the sufficiency of my evidence regarding damages on the grounds that damages under the FCRA *"cannot be recovered without a showing of actual loss."* To the contrary, the judge noted that courts have consistently held that *"actual damages may include humiliation and mental distress, even in the absence of out-of-pocket expenses. Here, the plaintiffs allege that they suffered emotional distress upon learning that Equifax has reported incorrect credit information to prospective creditors, and resulting from the denial of credit by BP Oil, as well as their lengthy effort to correct their credit reports."* In other words, the judge decided that the case could not be dismissed as Equifax wanted due to lack of evidence regarding my damages.

4. My case **DID** have enough merit to move on to trial

The judge decided that my legal team and I did present enough evidence to move on to trail. The summary judgment then was denied—in part.

Next, the judge had to decide whether the case would be eligible for a reward of *punitive damages*. In order to show that my case against Equifax merited punitive damages, I would have to prove their actions were malicious, willful or done with the intent to cause me distress. I believe I could have easily proven that to be the case. The judge, however, ruled differently.

5. There was not enough evidence to prove malice

The FCRA states that consumers may not sue creditors for furnishing false information by accident. This section (1681h(e)) provides *"...qualified immunity to consumer reporting agencies except as to false information furnished with malice or willful intent to injure."* I had to prove that Equifax

149

maliciously provided the false information on my credit report—with knowledge that it was false or with reckless disregard of whether it was false or not.

The judge found that *"...the plaintiffs fail to adduce any evidence showing that Equifax knew the plaintiffs' credit history it furnished was false or that it entertained actual doubt regarding the veracity of such information. Thus, the plaintiffs' defamation claim is preempted by the FCRA."*

This conclusion surprised me immensely. Our evidence included proof of letters and UDF forms Shawmut and Fleet both claimed they forwarded to Equifax. Equifax's stand was they never received them and further pointed the finger of blame at both Shawmut and Fleet. In my view, Equifax had more than enough reason to believe the data they were disseminating was in fact false.

6. There was not enough evidence to prove the violations were willful

To obtain punitive damages, I had to prove that the violations Equifax committed were willful or in conscious disregard for my rights. Generally, courts have allowed a willful noncompliance claim to proceed where a defendant's conduct involves willful misrepresentations or concealments. In other words, the CRA misrepresented or hid some or all of a credit report from a consumer. Or, a plaintiff must prove that the CRA had a dispute reinvestigation policy that they were aware infringed on consumer's rights under the FCRA.

The judge's decision was that I did not produce *"...sufficient evidence of willful noncompliance with the FCRA to survive this motion for summary judgment. There is no evidence to support a claim that Equifax willfully misrepresented or concealed any part of a credit report from the plaintiffs. Moreover, the plaintiffs do not allege that Equifax adopted its reinvestigation policies with knowledge, or reckless disregard, as to whether they contravened rights of consumers under the FCRA. Finally, the plaintiffs' contention that Equifax failed to correct an error in their credit reports after receiving several notices does not constitute evidence of a willful violation."*

7. The judge could not give us what we did not ask for

In the Judge's finding—*"the plaintiffs do not allege . . . reckless disregard . . ."*—it appears we never actually asked the judge to find them guilty of reckless disregard in our complaint, a crucial claim when seeking punitive damages. Basically, *a judge can not give you what you don't ask for.*

I remember the day Alan filed our response. Our deadline had been looming and it was a rush to file it at the courthouse to beat that crucial deadline. As I mentioned, there is a massive amount of paperwork created in a case with just one defendant, imagine the workload when the case has five defendants –all of whom retained a team of corporate attorneys with the benefit of a large pool of support staff to draw from. Remember: it's not a fair and equal playing field when seeking justice with corporate giants—not by a long shot.

I must stress again the importance of seeking attorneys well-versed and extremely knowledgeable with the FCRA and all other consumer protection acts in order to ensure you are utilizing all remedies available to you under the law. I cast no blame on my attorneys -whatsoever. It was their first FCRA case. My attorneys did the best they could with the limited resources they had access to. Do not try to take on a case by paying an hourly rate –either. Unlike my first case that caused me to pay my attorney hourly –this federal case was on a contingency basis –meaning my attorneys didn't get paid unless and until I received compensation (on a percentage basis –not hourly).

8. There was not enough evidence to prove intentional infliction of distress

Equifax was also trying to escape liability for intentional infliction of emotional distress in their summary judgment. To prevail on a such a claim, I had to establish: (1) that the defendant intended to inflict emotional distress, or knew or should have known that emotional distress was the likely result of its conduct; (2) the defendant's conduct was extreme and outrageous; (3) the defendant's actions caused my distress; and (4) the emotional distress I suffered was so severe that no reasonable person could be expected to endure it.

The judge had concluded earlier that my damages, including such emotional distress, were sufficiently sound to allow the case to move forward. However, he continued to conclude, *"There is no evidence in this case that Equifax acted with the intention to inflict emotional distress. In addition, there is no evidence that Equifax's conduct was extreme and outrageous. Accordingly, the Court grants Equifax's motion to dismiss the plaintiffs' claim of intentional infliction of emotional distress."*

9. Summary judgment was granted in part and denied in part

In the first part of the judge's decision, he stated that my case had enough merit to move on to trial. In other words, he did not let Equifax off the legal hook in terms of their responsibility and liability.

However, Equifax was also stating that I did not have enough evidence to be seeking punitive damages and, on this point, the judge sided with the defendant. According to the judge, *"In the absence of any evidence that Equifax acted to intentionally harm the plaintiffs, summary judgment must be granted as to this claim."*

My case against Equifax was allowed to move to a jury, but the denial of punitive damages meant Equifax no longer had to fear that the jury could award me hefty punitive damages.

That fear was replaced by an amazingly arrogant attitude. The removal of our ability to ask the jury for punitive damages also made it difficult, if not impossible, for this case to move forward. My (by now) ex-husband, no longer wanted to cooperate. His attitude was *"maybe she wants to proceed but I don't."* My attorneys believed that without my ex-husband's cooperation, along with having a judge – they viewed wanted this case to come to a close; my only realistic option was to settle.

On another important note, Equifax was the last remaining defendant. Had I either kept the CRA's all together in the case or if I didn't release and settle with Fleet, the result may have been very, very different.

Chapter 12 – *An Inconceivable Mess*

After settling with Equifax, I breathed a huge sigh of relief, believing the nightmares of courtrooms, depositions and corporate attorneys were safely behind me. My credit contained only accurate information and, after nearly 10 years, that was a major, major thing to me. I could finally begin the process of moving on. I never wanted to hear from Fleet or the credit bureaus, or see the inside of a courtroom again. As long as I continued to pay my bills on time and Fleet left me alone, as promised, the intrusive bad memories and lingering effects of stress would begin to fade. I was still suffering from some of this pent-up anxiety and I battled to get my health back. Having Equifax out of my life—15 months after moving to Florida—finally gave me a sense of freedom and took huge weights off my shoulders.

However, six months before settling with Equifax, I was still having health problems. Unfortunately, due to my move to Florida, my health insurance was only allowed coverage if I was seen in an emergency room. It didn't cover actual doctor's office visits yet, but fortunately, I had a friend I could turn to that was a physician and could prescribe the necessary antibiotics for a recurrent sinus infection. While taking the antibiotics, I soon realized I was suffering with an allergic reaction to the medication. I had enormous size welts that emerged into a case of full blown hives –all over my body. I realized the welts were moving up my neck to my face, and knew it was time to go to the emergency room. They took one look at me and asked why I waited so long seek medical assistance.

"We're concerned at the extent of the hives –and can't believe you waited this long to come in. It can be very dangerous." They quickly administered medication, shots and monitored me for a couple of hours, prior to letting me go home. Several months down the road, I received a notice from Inphynet of Broward County advising me that payment for my visit to the emergency room had been rejected by my insurance company, Blue Cross/Blue Shield. I immediately contacted Blue Cross to question why they would refuse payment for services that I clearly needed, and my insurance coverage allowed for. Then, I thought –I need to contact Inphynet to ensure this *"non-payment"* wasn't reported to the credit bureaus. A sense of fear poured over me as I contemplated derogatory information being inserted into my credit file yet again. The representative at BC/BS after hearing my complaint, very kindly asked, "Can I place you on hold and review your file?"

"Of course and thank you," I responded, hoping this could all go away.

"Hi Denise, this is Nicole," said the representative. "The bill was rejected because you are only covered for hospital visits. This bill was coded as a doctor's appointment. It states 'Physician's Office.'" I explained that the Doctor I saw was in the emergency room and it wasn't an office visit. "In that case," she continued, "they simply billed it wrong and if they re-submit it correctly, we will pay it. Let's see if we can get them on the phone and correct this right now."

"Great," I responded. She placed me on hold and came back within a minute or two to relay that she had Inphynet on the phone. The BC/BS representative explained the problem to them and promised payment if they re-submitted with the correct coding and notated on the bill the confirmation number she was about to provide to them. I chimed in immediately, "Has this been reported to the credit bureaus?"

"No," the Inphynet representative stated. "I will note that we are re-submitting this bill, so there is no need to worry." *Don't worry, worry, worry . . .*

Nicole then chimed in. "This may take a month or so to catch up once you re-submit, before you receive payment."

"No problem," said Inphynet. "Her file is notated." The date of that first notation was April 2002.

A couple of months went by and another notice came in the mail, dated June, 2002. I thought for sure it was confirmation they received their payment of the $223 they were attempting to be legitimately paid for. My heart started racing as I opened the envelope and read, "THIS IS YOUR FINAL STATEMENT. IF PAYMENT IS NOT RECEIVED IN OUR OFFICE WITHIN SEVEN DAYS, WE WILL PURSUE FURTHER ACTION."

A notice like that may seem to the average person like no big deal—but I was no longer just an average person, and probably never will be. Any thought of a creditor reporting false information to the credit bureaus immediately made my heart beat faster. I raced to pick up the telephone, trying to determine who I should contact first, Blue Cross or Inphynet, with one other frightening thought racing through my mind. "Oh God, don't let it be reported to the credit bureaus!" After coming off a ten year fight for accurate credit, there was one thing I learned; it was very easy for creditors to place information into your credit file at the speed of light, but it was a far different matter to have that same information removed. It was now a full year since the hospital visit and I still could not make this $223 bill disappear.

I decided to call Blue Cross because last time they initiated a three way call and perhaps that would be the easiest way to find out why I received this second notice. I reached another Blue Cross representative that reviewed the file and said, "Denise, I see where they were provided a confirmation number for payment but they never re-submitted the claim. Let's get them on the phone and find out why." While I was placed on hold, I couldn't help but think about what nerve Inphynet had to send me this notice. They would pursue further action if they didn't receive their funds within seven days yet they hadn't even re-submitted the bill as promised.

The Inphynet representative, Blue Cross and I were

all on the same line again. Again, promises were made by Inphynet to resubmit and they were provided with another confirmation number that would serve two purposes. First, it was proof that this call transpired and second, the number served as a promise from Blue Cross to pay the damn $223 bill. Once again, I had their assurance that this bill was not and would not be reported to the credit bureaus. BC/BS communicated the fact that it would take a month or two to catch up once re-submitted before they would receive their money.

"No problem, I have notated her file." The Inphynet rep reassured us. I couldn't help but feel great appreciation for Blue Cross's efforts in helping me to clear this up before it evolved into another nightmare on my credit reports. I thanked her immensely after Inphynet hung up their end, confiding in her what I had recently been through. Maybe I sounded paranoid, I said, but I had good reason to be. She kindly offered words of encouragement and relayed that all our conversations with Inphynet were documented. Their promises not to report to the credit bureaus were documented as well. Unfortunately, my life had been full of broken promises and it was not so easy for me to trust in them. At least the documentation and proof that the bill would be both paid and unreported to the credit bureaus was safely in the computer files of Blue Cross.

Don't worry, worry, worry . . .

I would soon find I had reason to worry, that echoing fear, again resurfaced when another notice dated July 30, 2002 arrived at my door from a company called IMBS. I contacted Blue Cross and spoke with Matt. Similar to the last representatives, he was very kind and supportive. After reviewing the notes contained in the files, he offered to contact IMBS, which I later found to be Inphynet's in-house collection agency. All three on the phone together, we went over the fact that their records indicated they had been supplied numerous confirmation numbers and promises that they would re-submit the bill with the correct coding but to date had not done so. Matt provided them with another

157

confirmation code as IMBS promised that this would be corrected and again confirmed it had not been reported to the credit bureaus. If anyone had read or heard my constant questioning about the credit bureaus without knowing my story, I'm sure they would think I had a colossal phobia or a touch of Obsessive Control Disorder. Perhaps they would be correct. I didn't know if it was a type of post-traumatic stress or simply that I had become all too acquainted with the stress and frustrations of trying to correct false and damaging information on a credit report.

The hot summer months were gone and the holidays were emerging. Florida's hurricane season had passed and unlike the most recent years, there were no major storms. Our beaches began to fill up with tourists and the air was void of that horrible humidity that instantly turns your hair into a ball of frizz. I was looking forward to my friends from home meeting the great friends I had met in Florida. I had now been living in Florida for two years and was successfully moving on with my life. Just when you think you can let your guard down, however, something jumps out of the blue to knock you back down and jolt you with a dose of reality.

The phone rang. "Hello, is this Denise Richardson?"

"Yes, this is she," I responded.

"I'm calling from IMBS Collections," a voice said, "in regards to a $223 bill you owe Inphynet." Those words were all I needed to hear before I felt my face heat up and my heart start racing.

"Not again. Collections?!" was all I could manage to get out of my mouth. "Did this get reported to the credit bureaus?"

I explained the entire set of circumstances and reminded them that Inphynet should never have placed this bill for collections.

"Do your records indicate how many times we have tried to correct the coding problem of the original bill from Inphynet?" I asked. "Do you realize it is now December of 2002 and you still can't correct your errors regarding a June

2001 medical bill of $223?" I got no response.

I was told that IMBS was Inphynet's in-house collection agency and Inphynet, the creditor, was a large corporation that serviced hospital facilities with their medical billings. The representative on the phone went on to tell me, after I demanded to know, that they do not report to the credit bureaus. "I do notice some confirmation numbers from Blue Cross to receive payment, but no notes on whether or not they were ever paid. Let me check with my supervisor and I will call you back if there is a problem," she said.

I didn't want to intrude on Blue Cross again, fearing they would eventually get sick of my calls and drop me as an insured. I would wait to hear back from her supervisor before doing so and just pray this would all go away.

January rolled around and along with it came another letter from IMBS. I hoped the contents would finally be a notice that they received their money or fixed their errors, but instead it was another notice of collection dated January 9, 2003. We were now edging close to the two year anniversary of the actual emergency room visit. Could this really be happening? Had I come full circle only to be on that old familiar ride again? *Fasten your seatbelt*, I thought, *and welcome back to the not-so–merry-go-round. Is there anyone out there willing to stop the ride and let me off? I think I am going to be sick.*

I quickly got a hold of Blue Cross and pleaded for their assistance. As a representative named Amanda reviewed all the documentation in her file, she relayed that a re-submitted bill did come in from Inphynet in August, 2002, but it contained the same inaccurate coding of their initial bill.

"They were notified that we [Blue Cross] were making a special exception to our policy of not paying bills this old," she continued, "but needed their assistance in submitting the bill with the correct coding. There have been repeated requests made for this information *because* it's necessary, in order to ensure the payment is processed and paid accurately." She bravely made the call to IMBS and then reported the results of her conversation to me.

Amanda explained "I told them this was a courtesy we did for them in allowing a one-time exception to pay this bill they didn't re-submit and I gave them another confirmation code. I also talked to them about your fears Denise that this bill could end up erroneously on your credit report and they again confirmed –they will not report it to the bureaus." I felt a sense of relief –and appreciation for her assistance.

"I told them if they did, they needed to ensure it was removed and reported to the CRAs as IMBS error," Amanda reassured me.

"I can't thank you enough for all your help Amanda. I just don't have faith this will ever go away."

"Don't worry, Denise. Their representative assured me that they had not reported this to the credit bureaus." She couldn't have known those words didn't soothe me.

A couple of weeks later I received my claim summary from Blue Cross which finally showed the bill was processed and actually paid. Halleluiah! The date of the explanation of benefits was dated January 21, 2003, and notated the account number with the date of service of June, 2001. Finally, I believed as Blue Cross believed, this bill for $223 would disappear. My life had begun to appear normal and a few months had gone by without one collection call – thankfully!

My girlfriend Judi flew in from Massachusetts for a long weekend. We quickly headed down to the beach for Friday night happy hour. While we were sitting at a local beach bar, in walked Michael Mac, a well-known Lieutenant on the Hollywood Beach Patrol. I had recently been introduced to him about a month or so earlier when we met through mutual friends on the beach.

He swaggered in along with a few guys and someone announced "It's Michael Mac's birthday!" Though his last name isn't "Mac" all who know of him, from here to the Jersey shore, rarely refer to him simply as Michael.

I had noticed him often riding around in his rescue

truck, appearing to oversee the lifeguards while also overseeing the beautiful girls on the beach! I had already labeled him a "player." *I want no part of this guy, as nice as he seems*, I thought, because player was clearly stamped on his forehead just above his bright blue eyes. He looked towards me and smiled and then turned to greet Judi.

"Hi, Michael Mac" he grinned with a beautiful, perfectly aligned, bright smile extending his hand to shake her hand. "It's my birthday and we're out celebrating."

"Really?" I asked.

"I just had my birthday six days ago."

"Hey Peggy, he turned to the bartender, I want to buy a round of drinks for us."

He sat next to me and kept staring at me and smiling- as if he knew something I didn't. We carried on a conversation for maybe an hour or so. I discovered he was a devoted Eagles fan and a loyal Jimmy Buffet (*parrot head)* follower. He was gregarious and easy to talk. Suddenly –he got up and announced he had to leave and said his good-byes. Less than a half an hour later he stormed back in through the doors, out of breath and disheveled, as if he had just run a race. He immediately walked up to me with a really serious look on his face and lined his eyes up to meet mine.

"I just ran all the way back here from my parking spot, *really* - about a mile away, because I *had* to come back to tell you something." I listened intently.

"I don't know why...and I know this will sound crazy...this isn't something I have ever done or said before, but *something* was pushing me back here to tell you something –really!"

"What Michael Mac?" I laughed.

"Really, I know this is going to sound crazy but I have to tell you...I had to come back and tell you..."

Before he got out another word –he moved another step closer, pointed at me and smiled.

"I know I'm going to marry you someday."

My response was abrupt –and contained only four

words...with laughter.

"*Ohhhkayyy*, you crazy person!" That was my instantaneous reaction. He didn't say another word he just turned around and flew out the door as quickly as he had flown in. As flattering as it sounded, I laughed it off because I didn't at all believe him and I *knew* I wasn't at all interested in any long-term or even a short-term relationship. As far as I was concerned, I was *especially* not interested in any man that I perceived to be "a player." I had been married to a man who turned out to be a player for just shy of 20 years and it caused a lot of unnecessary pain.

After that night, Michael would call my home and leave messages inviting me out to dinner. I never returned the calls. In fact, as I listened to the messages, right before I deleted them, I would hear myself saying out loud "Oh, no – that crazy guy again!" It took a few unreturned phone calls before he realized I was not going on a date with him –and soon the messages stopped. We continued to run into each other on the beach and I continued to tell him I wasn't dating. "That's not what I wanted to hear," he would say one Friday night, "but can we at least have a drink together if we run into each other?"

"Sure, no problem," I responded, feeling a sense of relief that I was totally up front with him about my dating situation, or lack thereof.

When we did have drinks together and friends asked if we were dating, my immediate response was, "No . . . we're just hanging out." Often, we'd be out at a local hangout on the beach and someone we knew would ask, "Are you two dating?" Whoever was sitting next to us knew the answer and would often pipe in to say, "No! They're just hanging out," and everyone would laugh –including Michael. But, on one particular Friday something started to change my mind about him. I was sitting on the beach and heard the noise of a vehicle traveling slowly on the "Broadwalk" and looked up to see Michael driving an ATV, a four-wheel drive apparatus used by the police and lifeguards, on the beach. By his side was a very tiny little girl in pigtails, peddling her tricycle with a smile on her face looking up at Michael. He appeared to be talking to her, keeping pace along side, and she seemed to be listening intently, moving her head back and forth from him to the tricycle's path.

We soon found out as word spread on the beach that a little girl was missing on "the broadwalk." (It's legally known as the *Broadwalk* purposely –because there are *no boards*—hence the traditional term boardwalk isn't used) It seems the little girl's mom was riding her bicycle with her and had a fall. The little girl, in the maze of people, continued on her ride and amazingly had traveled over a mile from the accident, unaware what happened to her mom.

Michael had found the little girl and was returning her to her mom who was with the police at the other end of the beach. When he got off duty he stopped by the outside beach bar where we were all gathered. Suddenly I realized that I now saw him through different eyes because of this small incident, a small incident that also revealed his large heart. I didn't know if that revelation was good or bad but it was enough for me to give him a chance and *think* about taking that first step—maybe a date...or at least we could "hang out" more –I thought.

Christmas was in the air and Michael called to ask me to the local Christmas parade on the beach. Again –I declined, but this time it wasn't because I wasn't interested – I just had other plans. The following weekend he invited me to a Christmas party at Sally and Jeff's house, which was technically our first date. He finally received that affirmative answer he had been persistently waiting for.

"What happened? I can't believe it took me three months to get you to go out on an actual date with me!"

As months flew by, life began showing signs of normalcy—no collectors calling, no disputes, no courtroom doors, and a great guy in my life that –continued to ask me almost daily to marry him! We had been exclusively dating for 9 months now but marriage was out of the question!

Just as in the past, however, all good things often come to an end. Michael was at my house when I received my mail one Saturday afternoon. I started going through the letters and found myself staring at an envelope that looked like a standard collection notice, the type that would always find their way to my mailbox to demand money I didn't owe. As I opened the envelope, I felt my heart beat picking up and my mind filling with fear. It was dated September 12, 2003 and the contents read in big, bold print:

Former Creditor: INPHYNET SOUTH
BROWARD, INC.

Balance due: $252.51

INPHYNET SOUTH BROWARD, INC. sold certain accounts owed to it, including the above mentioned account to MEDCLR, INC. NCO Financial Systems, Inc. is the servicer of this account . . . This is an attempt to collect a debt.

The account number on this notice was identical to the June, 2001 medical bill that Inphynet had already been paid for by Blue Cross. I couldn't believe my eyes. It was a bad dream that I couldn't wake up from, just like the Shawmut/Fleet/Credit Bureau catastrophe. Somehow this old, paid bill wouldn't go away. More humiliating though, was my need to explain the situation to Michael. It was embarrassing to have him see I was getting bill collector notices in light of the fact that I knew he was the type of person that writes the check the second he gets a bill in the mail—and it goes out the very next day. He was actually as obsessive as I was that his bills were paid on time to retain his excellent credit rating.

I explained the reason for my panic and tried to contact Blue Cross. Since it was a Saturday, I found their offices were closed and I needed to call on Monday. Monday came and I contacted Blue Cross again, feeling apologetic and uneasy about bothering them again. However, I was met with a kind and helpful voice on the other end. Blue Cross offered to assist me with my dispute by contacting NCO and provide them with the necessary information that would make them stop their collection attempts. Around this time, phone calls also began coming in from NCO and they weren't very nice calls –at all. I was basically belittled and screamed at in very rude and overly aggressive tone, *"Why don't you just pay the damn bill?"*

Melissa, my newest Blue Cross representative, promised me she would contact NCO after speaking to her supervisor about what she called "a nightmare that has gone on long enough." After much time on the phone, more letters of dispute, and exhaustive efforts by both Blue Cross and me, NCO agreed to accept BC/BS's explanation, and the proof that payment had been sent directly to the physician whose name was on the bill they submitted. Again, I received the normal assurances that this was not reported to the CRAs.

Eventually, BC/BS found through further research that the check they had cut and mailed back in January, nine months earlier, had not yet been cashed. They made numerous calls in an attempt to contact the physician's office where the check was mailed. Upon learning the check was never cashed the BC/BS supervisor said they would stop payment on it and send out another check, just to make this go away forever. I received another confirmation number from Blue Cross. "Denise," a representative named Wendy said, "we have all our conversations logged with confirmation numbers and notes so if you ever need our assistance, feel free to call. I have never seen anything like this. NCO representatives were not only rude, they were uncooperative and even hung up on me. They claim they didn't report this to the credit bureaus and I am noting all this in my log."

Silence and peace of mind lasted about one month before the next notice dated <u>October 22, 2003</u> from NCO arrived in my mail. The dollar amount they were now seeking was $253.98 and they now had the following claim: *We have been authorized by the above referenced creditor, INPHYNET to accept $165.09 as a lump sum of the above* *amount so long as payment is received within 30 days of the date of this letter.* More demanding and rude phone calls began coming into my home on a regular, annoying and intrusive basis. I told them if they hadn't already received the second check Blue Cross sent out, it would be there any day and they should contact BC/BS directly.

In <u>February 2004</u>, I got a call out of the blue from a company called Gold Key informing me they were a collection company trying to collect a debt for a medical bill from June 2001. Yes, that's right; the call came again in February, 2004. Guess who their client was –NCO! Totally frustrated, I went into the whole explanation and yet again got BC/BS on the phone with us. During that conversation the woman at Gold Key was extremely rude to both BC/BS and me. Therefore, BC/BS said they would make calls themselves and call me back.

Michelle from Blue Cross called, sounding very anxious, saying she had just gotten off the phone with a Gold Key representative. She stated emphatically...

"Denise, I will make it my mission to get this corrected. After reading everything documented, I can't believe how long we have been going through this. Plus, I have never dealt with such rude people as I did with their representatives. They would not allow me to speak with a supervisor nor would they give me anyone in management. All they would give me was a fax number, no address, to send them proof of payment."

She told me she documented their conversation and uncooperativeness. She also faxed them a letter with proof that the check was cleared on November 23, 2003, and that it was in fact the second check that Blue Cross had sent. She forwarded me a copy of what she provided them.

"I also called Inphynet," she insisted. "This should do it, Denise. The check has cleared and they have again received the documentation but...unfortunately...they *did* report this debt to Equifax...and reported it as a collection."

"Oh my God! Not the credit bureaus, are you sure?

"Yes, that's what they told me."

I immediately knew what had to come next. More disputes and more problems. I requested copies of my credit report and waited to receive the dreaded news. While I was waiting for the credit report, I received my latest credit card statement. I reviewed the statement and saw that my interest rate had shot up to an unimaginable 28%. I thought it had to be an error and immediately contacted my credit card company.

"I have been a loyal card holder of yours since the late 80s. I have never, *ever* missed a payment and never have I been late. Can you tell me why my credit line has been lowered and my interest rate has sky rocketed to an amount of interest I didn't even know was legal?"

"Sure, Ms. Richardson, let me look at your file," the credit card representative said. "Well, all I am allowed to tell you is that it was due to something reported in your Equifax report. Our system is set up to automatically review our cardholders' accounts monthly and something must have come up on your credit report." I told her I knew what it was. There was only one possible thing it could be—that $200 plus medical bill finally made its way on my report. It was obviously reported even after they had cashed the check from Blue Cross. I explained this but to no avail. She said there was nothing they could do about it because their policy is across the board—they make no exceptions. "You can dispute it and if they take it off when we review your account next month, your interest rate will automatically be adjusted or you can call us," she concluded.

"This is a common practice" she said, "it's called data sharing and we review all of our customers' information on a regular basis."

"Given the fact that credit reports—are notoriously inaccurate, don't you have procedures in place that can take into account that you may be basing your decision to raise an innocent consumer's interest rate on dirty data?" I had no doubt this interest rate hike was based on inaccurate information.

This couldn't have happened at a worse time.

Fulfilling the out-of-his-ordinary prophesies from the night we first met, Michael, proposed to me (on bended-knee) on Christmas night-2003. It was just a year after our first date.

Maybe he wasn't the "crazy person" that I originally believed he was on that serendipitous night.

Whatever the reason for it, Michael and I were now engaged and soon we began talking about our future plans – selling our individually owned properties and buying a home together. Here we were, about to buy a new home together and now my credit rating was basically destroyed.

About the same time this notice came in, we had recently found the home we wanted to purchase. I had to somehow explain to Michael that my credit was once again damaged goods.

"Remember that old medical bill honey and bogus collection account I told you about? Well, it never died. It was just smacked on my credit report by a collection company and now my credit is a mess –again."

I showed him proof the bill was paid and proof they were continuing to destroy my credit. Michael was shocked, as is everyone who has never lived through this type of nightmare. Michael never had to deal with inaccurate credit reporting and had no clue how devastating it can be once you've become a target. That's how I felt—I had a target painted on my back that was irresistible to credit and collection agencies. It was now one quarter of the way through 2004 and yet there appeared to be no end in sight.

My fears began to build that I would be forced into the court system to get it to go away because now I had my biggest fear come true—the error, in which I had no fault, was reported on my credit and was already costing me money due to this latest interest rate hike. I knew the FCRA had provisions to protect my rights for fair and accurate credit reporting but I needed to know more about the FDCPA (The Fair Debt Collection Practices Act). It can appear complex but I found an easy to understand description of the FDCPA written by Barbara Woodcox, founder of Consumercity.org. Barbara, a long time consumer advocate, receives and answers hundreds of letters from consumers who are seeking an explanation of various consumer rights. In these days with growing concerns for identity theft and the realization that our credit data is often inaccurate... or if you've ever had bill collectors calling you demanding money they claim you owe, then you need to know your rights under the Fair Debt Collection Practices Act (FDCPA).

1. It is illegal for debt collectors to make <u>false statements</u>. It is illegal for them to do any of the following:

- Misrepresent the amount of money you owe

- Imply that they represent the government or any law enforcement agency

- Imply that they are attorneys if they aren't attorneys

- Imply that you have committed a crime or will be arrested (owing a debt is a civil matter, not criminal)

- Imply or state that they are affiliated with the credit bureaus

- Lead you to believe that papers they send are legal forms when they're not

- Lead you to believe that legal papers sent to you are not legal forms

- Threaten you with legal proceedings without cause or intention (idle threats)

- Threaten to take your property or wages if it isn't legally feasible and they have no intention of doing so (idle threats)

- Make false statements about you to anyone. No exceptions!

- Send you items made to look like court papers when they're not

- Send you papers made to look like they are from the government when they're not

- Use a false name

2. It is illegal for debt collectors to <u>harass and annoy</u> you. It is illegal for them to do any of the following:

- Threaten you with any kind of harm to yourself, to people you know, to your reputation or to your property

- Call you on the telephone excessively to wear you down and cause you to give in to their demands

- Use offensive language

- Publish your name in any source as a person owing a debt. The only exception is reporting to the credit bureaus.

- Call before 8:00 AM or after 9:00 PM—in your time zone, not theirs

- Call you at work after you or your employer told them not to

- Tell other people about your debt. The exceptions are your spouse or attorney. If you are a minor, your parents can also be told.

3. It is illegal for debt collectors to use <u>unfair practices.</u> It is illegal for them to do any of the following:

- Persuade you to accept charges for telegrams or collect calls

- Cash your post-dated check earlier than the date on the check

- collect an amount that is more than you owe, unless allowed by your state's laws

- Contact you if your attorney has contacted them or if they know how to contact your attorney

- Refuses to honor your Dispute or Cease Communication Rights

You need to know your rights under the FDCPA. You have the right to dispute the validity of the debt. Within 5 days after they first contact you, the debt collector is required to send a letter that includes information on how to dispute the debt. This letter is usually a typical collection letter with the part about your rights at the bottom, on the back, or written with a much lighter ink than the rest of the letter. If you write to the collection agency telling them that you dispute the debt and that you request validation of the debt in writing, they must stop contacting you until they mail the validation. However, you must send a written request for validation within 30 days of receiving the letter described above if you want them to stop contacting you until you get the validation. NOTE: If you don't dispute the debt within 30 days, it is not an admission that you owe the money.

It is highly recommended that you communicate with debt collectors only by certified mail. It's not against the law to hang up on debt collectors when they call.

You have the right to tell a debt collector to cease all communication with you. If you do this, they can only contact you to tell you what their next action will or might be. They can no longer harass you. However, if the debt is legitimate, they can still use any legal remedy they see fit to collect the debt. In other words, the FDCPA cannot be used to eliminate legitimate debts.

As soon as I got off the phone, I immediately faxed both Equifax and Mr. Jim Bailey, the manager of Gold Key, 12 pages containing all the pertinent information along with a letter explaining what transpired. I insisted on the removal of this erroneous debt, insisted that he call me to confirm he received the fax, and that he promptly take care of it. I enclosed a copy of the letter from Blue Cross clearly stating that the check cleared with all the pertinent dates and account number, etc. The one constant during the chaos of this medical billing disaster was that the date of service and account number had never been changed. That should have made it easy enough for the credit bureaus and the collection agencies to clean up their debacle stop reporting this non-existent debt and stop all attempts at collection.

Why weren't their so-called "procedures" intended to stop these abusive actions from happening –working?

Jim Bailey finally returned my calls. He said he wanted to make sure this was cleared up as soon as possible and asked me to forward a few more pieces of information. I spent *hours* pulling it all together and then sent it via fax directly to his attention. After researching everything I sent him he called and proclaimed –yes, he agreed with me the debt was in fact paid! "After all you have been through," he said, "we are going to waive the $5 co-pay balance for you."

"I will gladly send the $5 if you give me an address," I said, eager to do anything to end the situation.

"No need. We've waived the $5 charge and all is settled. I apologize for the inconvenience and assure you that we've reported our error to the credit bureaus. Don't worry." Right –don't worry? He had no clue those words didn't stop my worries, rather they just intensified them. I didn't trust him or the credit bureaus. It was now <u>March 19th 2004</u> and it was nearing the three-year anniversary of that fateful emergency room visit. April rolled in and just as we were getting ready to move into our new home, along with it came a letter from Equifax containing the results of their investigation. Just as I had seen so many times over the last ten years, there were the same words that had been blazoned across my report throughout the last decade:

> "We have researched the credit account #INPHYNET -1869. The results are as follows: **Equifax has verified that this item has been reported correctly**. Additional information has been provided from the original source regarding this item. If you have additional questions about this item please contact:
>
> Medclr, PO Box 8547, Philadelphia PA"

The details of the "verification" read as follows:

Date reported: June, 2004
Balance amount: $263.00
Date of Last Activity: 01/2004
Date Opened: 08/2003
High Credit: $223.00
Account #: Inphynet *1869
Current Status: Over 120 days Past Due
Type of account: Open
Collection Account

That Post Office Box listed above (and in Equifax's verification) is the same postal address as NCO's. Well, does that appear to you that my troubles are over? Do you see any end in sight? Does this surprise you or boggle your mind? Imagine, if you can, the sense of powerlessness a consumer feels when constantly told dirty data has been verified as clean and accurate. This **paid** medical bill of June, 2001 was essentially *verified* as a **debt due**. All the proof I had would not let it die—it just wouldn't end. It felt like I was in a time warp as the events of the past flooded my thoughts and all I had been through in the past came rushing back to me. My old virtual tenants from hell that took over my life for so long were pounding on my doors to move back in. I wanted to enjoy my life, plan my wedding and excitedly move into my new home with Michael. I did not, at any cost want them moving in with me. I had lost too much time and already paid too high of a price. My adversaries' invasive intrusions into my life caused chronic stress, physical ailments, and –as I have seen so many times, directly contributed to the destruction of my 20-year marriage.

This time, they were not going to take over my life. Perhaps someone that hadn't lived through a decade of battles to get back their true credit identity would have been less upset, but this situation began to panic me—yet again.

Chapter Lesson: Secrets, Lies and Red Tape

The actual number of consumer complaints reported to the Federal Trade Commission is a very closely guarded secret. Even under the Freedom of Information Act, the FTC will not make those numbers public. However, there seems to be a magic number they must hit before they will step in on our behalf to investigate bad behavior and enforce the consumer protection laws. When consumers were complaining they were unable to get through to the credit bureaus when trying to reach them by telephone, there must have been enough complaints to make the FTC act. This settlement notice was released on the FTC site on January 13, 2000:

**Nation's Big Three Consumer Reporting
Agencies Agree To Pay $2.5 Million to
Settle FTC Charges of Violating Fair
Credit Reporting Act**

Three national consumer reporting agencies, Equifax Credit Information Services, Inc., (Equifax), Trans Union LLC (Trans Union), and Experian Information Solutions, Inc. (Experian), have agreed to a total of $2.5 million in payments as part of settlements negotiated by the Federal Trade Commission to resolve charges that they each violated provisions of the Fair Credit Reporting Act (FCRA) by failing to maintain a toll-free telephone number at which personnel are accessible to consumers during normal business hours. According to the FTC's complaints, Equifax, Trans Union and Experian (collectively, consumer reporting agencies or CRAs) blocked millions of calls from consumers who wanted to discuss the contents and possible errors in their credit reports and kept some of those consumers on hold for unreasonably long periods of time. The proposed settlements with each CRA also would require that it meet specific performance standards to ensure that CRA personnel are accessible to consumers.

The FTC does not assist individuals but rather, they step in to stop any abuses when they receive a set number of complaints that indicated a pattern of abuse. No one at the FTC was willing, or perhaps able, to tell me what that magic number was. How many complaints did it take to spur them into action to investigate our claims? Why is the tallied number of complaints against these corporations as secret as their scoring recipe? Why is it considered classified data?

The FTC *is* the enforcement agency that oversees complaints about the credit reporting industry- yet they are completely incapable of dealing with reducing the effects and growth of identity theft. They appear understaffed and overwhelmed, but their inability to respond to our individual requests for investigations, or even lend assistance directly to individuals, makes it even more crucial that we have state and federal laws that we can turn to in our time of need. Case in point: HR 3997;

This proposed bill was sponsored by Rep. Steve LaTourette (R-OH). LaTourette has spun this bill to be viewed as a consumer protection measure; giving it the name *The Financial Data and Security Act.* But in reality it is the "worst data bill ever" as summed up by US PIRG. The bill's given name is simply a rouse designed to slip by the American public's eyes, disguised as a consumer protection measure. When the bill is dissected and the smoke and mirrors are removed anyone can clearly see *something* isn't right. HR3997 would strip away our rights and render our state laws useless.

More than a dozen states have passed laws that give consumers some ability to freeze their credit file. In every state that allows credit freezes, the laws offer better protection and are significantly stronger than HR 3997. The bill, which only allows consumers to freeze their credit file *after* they have become victims of identity theft, also limits a consumer's ability to file law suits. Why is a credit freeze helpful to consumers who have been put at risk by data breaches? Here's why... a credit freeze can abort an identity theft and stop it dead in its tracks. Creditors can't run credit checks without obtaining your permission which then leaves the identity thief unable to obtain credit. When they render our state protection laws useless it takes away our much needed measures of protection, when we need them most. At least 30 states have effective data breach notification laws requiring companies that store data on consumers, to notify consumers when their data is stolen, breached or accessed by unauthorized parties.

Businesses that fail to notify consumers that a data breach occurred have been faced with stiff fines and other penalties.

If HR 3997 becomes law, all of the states data breach laws currently on the books will be gone. While the current situation is bad, this new legislation seems to be recipe for disaster!

A few more tidbits: Consumers are often unaware that corporations such as the CRA's and NCO "outsource" many jobs to other continents. In fact, NCOs' website boasts to their perspective clients that their "outsourcing" provides cost savings in that; *"NCO can reduce labor costs 30 to 70%, decreasing overall net process costs by 20 to 50%. Utilizing offshore resources contributes to cost savings."* Their website proudly boasts *"NCO operates an international network of over 100 customer contact centers,"* which include India, Panama, Barbados, Philippines, Puerto Rico, and Canada, to name a few. Often our requests for investigations and actual verifications of our complaints are done outside the United States. For example, Equifax, who in my case proved to be the most difficult of the "big three" to deal with, subcontracts out most of its consumer relations. Telephone disputes or requests are diverted to a Canadian company and mailed disputes or requests for investigations that we send to their Georgia address are simply scanned to a computer file and then electronically sent to a subcontract vendor either in Jamaica or the Philippines.

Equifax in particular has been the subject of intense FTC scrutiny. In 1995, an FTC Consent Decree found that Equifax *"failed to assure the maximum possible accuracy of consumer credit information . . . Specifically, when a consumer provides Equifax with documentation confirming the consumer's version of a dispute, Equifax is required to accept that version unless it has reason to doubt the authenticity of the document."* This decree reiterated that Equifax was required to *"implement procedures to assure that no derogatory information which has been deleted, after being disputed by the consumer, reappears on the consumer's credit report unless (1) the information has been re-verified, and (2) Equifax advises the consumer in writing that the information has been reinserted in the credit file."* When the FTC issues such an order, it carries the force of law and each violation could result in a fine of up to $10,000.00

I would love to know what changes they've made to their procedures and what exactly they have done to "fix" their obvious systemic problems. I could clearly see that their procedures were still flawed by simply reading the results of their latest so-called investigation. It appears that not only did they shun the FTC's order to implement specific changes but apparently their staff couldn't keep up with consumer complaints as indicated by another fine by the Federal Trade Commission (FTC)

For Release: July 30, 2003 ftc.gov

Equifax to Pay $250,000 to Settle Charges

FTC Alleges Blocked and Delayed Consumer Calls Violated Consent Decree

Equifax Credit Information Services, Inc. (Equifax) will pay $250,000 to settle Federal Trade Commission charges that its blocked-call rate and hold times violated provisions of an FTC consent decree that settled a 2000 lawsuit for violations of the Fair Credit Reporting Act (FCRA). That lawsuit settled charges that Equifax did not have sufficient personnel available to answer the toll-free phone number provided on consumers' credit reports.

Equifax failed to meet the specific performance standards in the consent decree for blocked calls and hold times for certain periods in 2001. The settlement announced today will require Equifax to pay an additional $250,000 for violating the original consent decree.

Chapter 13 – *Mortgage Mania*

Moving, it is said, can be the most stressful event in one's life. I agree with this theory whole-heartedly. It seemed like a monumental task yet, in the middle of all the collection mess, we still found a way to sell two homes, buy a new one, and merge the contents of our two lives into one, all while managing to remain together.

Unlike my last battle for my credit identity, I wasn't going to allow these new demons to take over my life, my health, or my personal relationships. I made myself push those issues to the back burner after completing another dispute form. I wasn't Superwoman, able to handle the merging of my life with Michael's and deal with my nemesis, Equifax. Therefore, I contacted all involved, re-submitted my disputes and simply waited to hear the results. We had purchased the home in April and moved in around the middle of May, 2004. In June, we received a notice from our mortgage company informing us that our mortgage had been sold, advising us that we would soon be hearing from the new lender with instructions on where to send future payments. Soon after that notice, we received the letter they alluded to from our *new* bank. I opened the envelope and felt something flutter to the floor, coming to a rest on my foot. My eyes looked down and I realized what it was. I felt a lump in my throat as I bent down, in what felt like slow motion, to pick it up. There it was—our new payment coupon book. It was as if all the ghosts of my past were coming back to haunt me, jumping out from behind corners to shout, "BOO!"

Michael was aware of the medical bill problems but not the details of the past - what I had been through over the last 13 years. I rarely, if ever spoke of it. In fact none of my friends here in Florida were aware of what I had been through, except for a few that found my name on the internet when seeking guidance for their own credit problems. I sat him down to explain that all my troubles began with my inability to verify how my payments were applied due to the use of this ominous payment coupon book which was the push that caused that first key domino to fall. I needed him to understand where I was coming from and why this affected me so deeply. I also needed to warn him that he shouldn't send in any additional principal payments without receiving proof of *how* the money was applied.

"I'll call the new mortgage servicing company and ask if we can get monthly statements."

"We can't send everyone a monthly statement. Do you know how much that would cost?" was the response I received when I called and reached the first representative.

"No," I replied, "but I do know that other banks offer statements and companies such as our electric company, credit card companies and utility companies send monthly statements. They can afford it," I snapped back.

"As long as you send in your payments on time every month you have nothing to worry about."

Oh, right! Sure!

"Well," I responded. "That is easy for you to say because you haven't walked in my shoes. I just got through a ten year battle that all began by tearing out a coupon to send in with my payment. Why would I trust that things would be any different this time?"

"I'm sorry for you," she said, without sounding it, "but we can't provide monthly statements."

My predictions of future troubles arising from using a payment coupon book seemed as if they were as true as Michael's prophesy of marriage. It only took a couple of months before my prediction became a reality. In mid-November, we received a notice in the mail from our new mortgage company telling us they hadn't received our November 1st payment. I knew they had to be wrong because Michael wrote the mortgage check out every month—early. He's obsessive about paying his bills the second they arrive in the mail, as opposed to writing out his checks all in one sitting prior to their due dates. I went through his statements and there it was—proof the check had cleared and was deducted from his account. I contacted the bank immediately and relayed that they were mistaken. The bank statement showed the check made payable to them was in fact cashed.

"Just fax or mail us a copy of the statement and a copy of the cancelled check. We will take care of it," they said. The next morning, Michael went to his credit union and paid for copies of the front and back of the cleared check. As soon as he dropped them off -I faxed the proof of payment to the bank within seconds! Later that afternoon, I contacted the bank to find out if they received my fax and to confirm they would correct their error.

"Yes," I was assured.

"We received everything so, don't worry, we'll take care of it." *Don't worry? Laughable!*

As in the past, I turned to the web to research mortgage servicing problems caused or exacerbated by consumers who were unable to track their payments and verify where there money was going when they sent in monthly payments. I found myself on a site called www.msfraud.org, short for mortgage servicing fraud. I was horrified, truly horrified by the stories I read. People were losing their homes when they did nothing wrong. People were having their lives torn apart and their houses stolen out from under them, again, for doing nothing wrong. People were in long term battles, sometimes lasting years and then still losing their homes through illegally forced foreclosures. These borrowers did have a common thread though –they were blindly trusting that their bank was applying their payments accurately.

I had learned not to blindly trust that banks were responsible and trustworthy long ago. In 1995, when I testified before the Massachusetts Banking Commission on the merits of S16 and the need for a "checks and balance" system in the form of monthly statements, I never imagined that by moving to a different state I would be forced into using coupon books a decade later. How was it possible that banks were still getting away using coupon books that masked any accounting problems or fraud? The reasons, I thought, were many. Yet it scared me immeasurably when I stumbled across the msfraud.org website and read in horror that fraud had grown by leaps and bounds and nobody seemed to care. Consumers were on their own, trying to hold onto their homes while fighting illegal foreclosures when they hadn't done anything wrong. Worse, it seems that when they found a local reporter to speak out about their individual nightmares, suddenly the stories were pulled from websites and reporters would mysteriously not be working for the same station anymore. It became clear that advertising dollars spoke louder than the outraged cries of a wronged consumer.

I spoke with many of the victims who contacted me (or I contacted) after reading their stories. One of the people whose personal struggles seemed all too eerily similar to mine is a consumer named Jack. As I read his story, I saw that he had experienced the same creditor tactics and long-lasting effects as I had, which left him battling for nearly a decade to hold on to his dream home. Throughout Jack's battle, we've kept in touch by phone and talked at length. We realized that we both shared many similar feelings of powerlessness. Knowing how widespread and damaging the effects of mortgage fraud are on innocent families, we found we had many relatable frustrations and heard countless similar stories. Whether it is from fraud, corruption, negligence, weak consumer protection laws, or inaccurate credit reporting, we knew and understood the ramifications of what we have been forced to deal with. It had seeped into every area of our lives -even though neither of us ever could have predicted it. We felt like we ate, breathed and slept our nightmares, which validated and reassured us, (as did the stories of so many other victims); we were far from being alone. We were only deceptively portrayed as unique cases by the industry in a calculated attempt to make these problems appear that they were not systemic.

I couldn't help but realize from my many conversations with Jack, that he had paid a steep price and endured many personal losses, simply because he trusted his mortgage company. His nightmare could be a nightmare that *anyone* could find themselves living. There are many of us who "get it," *only* because of what we have lived through. However, we realize there are still so many uninformed consumers who couldn't be expected to "get it" without having walked in our shoes. Yet, unless there are major changes within the industry and better consumer protection laws implemented, I fear others will soon inevitably find themselves walking this tragic path of destruction without having done anything wrong.

Jack's story below illuminates the lengths to which these corporations will go in an attempt to either steal your home or hide any illegal activity that transpired. His story details corruption and ill-gotten gains within the financial, judicial and government sectors. All of this is very well-documented yet Jack couldn't get anyone to effectively stop it. To illustrate the egregiousness of this case, with Jack's permission, I am including a portion of his 9 year battle written in his words on May 1, 2006.

> When the mortgage company I have been litigating against realized I had the evidence to expose their criminal enterprise, they hired one of the most powerful law firms in the world, to their legal team to make sure it remained silent (at least in my view).

> My story begins in 1997, when a mortgage company tried to illegally foreclose on my home, claiming I missed one payment. Despite overwhelming evidence to the contrary, the courts always sided with the mortgage company without requesting proof of their allegations. When my legal expenses exhausted my life savings, I took my case *pro*

se to the Court of Appeals, the Supreme Court and the Supreme Court of the United States.

My case was revived in 2002 after a large law firm saw my story on the local ABC News. For the reporter's 5th segment, they followed me to the Capitol to report on my requested testimony before the Finance Committee. A short time later, while still investigating, the station pulled my story and the investigative reporter's employment was terminated. In 2004, I learned of the station's affiliation with my mortgage company's parent company, a Wall Street giant.

In December 2004, my case finally made it to trial. During this *partial* trial, the mortgage company finally confessed they did not own my home, as repeatedly claimed in court pleadings, depositions and hearings. The company representative also testified: **I was *never* in default; I had overpaid my escrow; and they had intentionally tried to steal my home and equity.** These shocking admissions meant every errant court ruling against me over many years were now null and void. With the truth and my innocence on record— my nightmare looked like it was finally coming to an end. (I was dead wrong and about to watch this criminal enterprise demonstrate unbridled control of the courts.)

Visibly jolted by their witness's testimony, the defense team had to come up with a sure-fire plan to get rid of the damaging testimony, the judge, my attorney and myself. Rather than rule on these admissions and the evidence we presented, the judge instead stopped the trial right before I took the stand and was <u>ordered</u> to a fourth mediation to settle with a defendant who just admitted being a fraud and who destroyed my life out of sheer greed.

The judge later recused herself; my attorney's ethics board forced him to withdraw, and I ended up at a mental hospital with extreme anxiety/panic attacks and suicidal thoughts. To date, no one has been able to get the court transcript proving my innocence.

When I refused to sign the mortgage company's demands allowing them to escape accountability, I was repeatedly lied to and held against my will for another 12 hours until I *wrote* my name on *some* documents. I became so ill that dying became far more appealing than what I was being forced to do, and I spent most of my time wondering if I had enough strength to jump out the 14th floor window. The only thing I could think of was to ask the court to intervene. Three months later, I was before a new judge who *refused* to approve the unconscionable demands and ordered my case "back to trial."

The mortgage company then filed suit against me for breach of contract. Nine months later, this same retired judge—for reasons unknown—granted the mortgage company a partial summary judgment. The judge did not read the alleged contract because the mortgage company refuses to allow the court or anyone, including myself, to view it.

Last July, we met with, and presented a portion of, our evidence to the Federal Trade Commission in Washington.

They are still trying to steal my home, and I do not know who can stop this. All I have left is the TRUTH. For updates and more information see msfraud.org.

Jack, who is completely innocent and has proven it, has now spent nine pain-filled years fighting to simply live in his home in peace. He has contacted his legislators, the regulatory agencies (whose duty is to protect us), and even journalists. To date, he still struggles to wake up from his nightmare while praying to hold onto his dream home. Is this really the American way? What happened to us?

Chapter Lesson: Mortgage Servicing *and* Fraud

Mortgage servicing fraud can happen on many levels and in many ways. In today's mortgage market, the home buyer is forced to deal with an incredibly complex process involving several businesses and dozens of people. A "loan servicer" becomes responsible for a number of important functions, not the least of which is applying the proper amounts to principal, interest, escrow, and such. As we discussed, over the life of the loan, servicing can be transferred (sold) several times and the borrower has no control over these transfers whatsoever. With many of the more creative loans made today, and rampant predatory lending schemes, the potential for errors and fraud on the part of the servicer is very high. Too often, homeowners don't find out about these problems until they seek to refinance, sell the home or worse, the servicing company starts making almost inexplicable demands, threatening foreclosure action unless their calls for fees and payments are met.

The more aggressive of these servicing companies (better known as lenders) will take advantage of these situations to profit from excessive, even illegal fees and force borrowers into costly forbearance or reinstatement agreements. While the FTC has stepped in and taken action on various companies assessing hefty fines, (one of the worst with a $55 Million-dollar settlement) forcing them to adopt more acceptable servicing practices, the settlement rulings have not stopped others who continue to take advantage of their almost unlimited power. Many situations where victims of servicing abuse were taken advantage of came about because the consumer didn't know the payments they were making were not being processed, turned over to the new servicer or accounted for properly until it was too late.

Why? Because some mortgage (servicing) companies either don't send a detailed, itemized monthly statement or they use pre-printed payment coupon books. Suddenly, the credit report starts showing past due amounts and late payments accrued without the consumer having knowledge their payment wasn't received from the prior servicer (lender). Just one of these easily manufactured late payments can prevent a borrower from getting refinancing, especially at their deserved rate of interest.

Many people have lost their homes to well-designed mortgage "servicing" scams that cannot be stopped without incurring enormous legal expenses. Rest assured that making payments on time does not prevent it from happening. There are companies in the mortgage business, that in my opinion, are deliberately keeping borrowers from taking advantage of lower interest rates by reporting erroneous credit data to the credit bureaus, leaving them unable to refinance.

The importance of accurate credit data reporting and scoring cannot be underestimated. It is crucial to profitability and continued growth for lenders and insurers. Negative reports effectively create a sub-prime class of consumers that must then be subjected to paying higher interest rates, insurance premiums and hefty Private Mortgage Insurance costs. Could that be one of the reasons the industry fights so hard to keep consumers from being able to effectively control their credit information—to continue to receive these higher fees? The borrower is essentially a prisoner and the *only* key continues to remain in the hands of the mortgage company. As in Jack's case and countless others, illegal foreclosures are manufactured by unscrupulous lenders and such schemes are so despicable that many of us never would suspect something like this could *really* ever happen. We assume, incorrectly, that no one would get away with it. The FTC and HUD are investigating some of the worst cases but the industry is using its enormous financial leverage and lobbying power to prevent the possibility of any new legal or regulatory barriers from being placed in their way.

When un-reputable lenders complain that a monthly statement would be too costly, we don't have to look too far to see why. Read between the lines. I don't think it's the price of a stamp, or the paper it's printed on, they're worried about. Rather, they may be worried that consumers that review their statements would be knowledgeable of the accrual of improper fees, erroneous late charges and misapplied payments. Responsible lenders and servicing companies should know and welcome the value of having informed consumers. I question the motives of those who want to leave consumers in the dark.

Chapter 14 – *Happy Holidays . . . or not?*

A busy holiday season was on us and we were planning a Christmas Eve party for 75 or so family and friends. Michael's Christmas Eve party had always been a much anticipated annual event—it was his ritual, but this year it would be in our new home. Early November Michael began to gear up for Christmas –and worked endlessly building his much loved outdoor light display. Christmas music filled the house, loud enough for him (and the neighbors) to hear, while he moved from inside and out as he gathered all his lights. During Christmas season, I refer to Michael as "Clark Griswold," the character Chevy Chase played in the movie *National Lampoon's Christmas Vacation.* Michael is like Clark—the more light strands that drape the house the better, and with Florida's warm weather, decorating is done while wearing shorts and flip flops. While it's his favorite time of the year, I never *really* enjoyed it. Instead, the season seemed stressful and I usually looked forward to it ending. Michael's exuberance, however, was bringing me around. He made it fun again, like when I was a young child without responsibilities.

As the recurrent pattern of this book can testify, when all seems good, it can often just be a mirage. It was December 1st, 2004, and at least six weeks had passed since Michael mailed our November 1st mortgage payment, mailing it in around the 23rd of October. It was also now a couple of weeks after I had faxed the bank the necessary proof that it was in fact paid. Yet, the phone rang at 5:30 pm.

"There's a man on the other end of the phone asking for you," I yelled to Michael as he was just getting in the door from work. I handed Michael the phone. I couldn't hear what the man on the other end was saying but I saw Michael's confusion on his face.

"Here," he said. "Talk to Denise. I know she faxed the information you asked for...here talk to her."

"Hello," I said hesitantly. "This is Denise."

"Denise, we did some research on the cancelled check you forwarded and we found that we didn't cash that check. In fact, it seems Comcast Cable cashed that check and we cashed a Comcast Cable check."

My mind started racing in an attempt to figure this out. "Can I ask you a few questions?" I said into the phone.

"Sure," he responded.

"Why did it take six weeks for you to discover this?

The letter I received in the mail stated; "*We have not received any payments since your last payment of October 1st.*"

Where did the $54 cable payment go to if, as you say, you cashed Comcast's check?"

I took a deep breath and continued,

"It is now December 1st, which officially makes our payment 30 days late. If I pay it over the phone right now, can I stop any computer generated report to the credit bureaus that would indicate we were late when we actually were informed by you that the bank had received all you needed from us?"

My mind kept leaping ahead with anger at the injustice of the whole situation.

"If what you are telling me is true, it's clear that Michael inadvertently placed the Comcast check in your envelope and accidentally sent the mortgage payment off in the Comcast envelope. How is it possible that both you and Comcast were able to cash these checks?"

"Well," the representative slowly replied, "It took a while for our research to come back. We did cash your Comcast check but we took $25 for a late fee and the other $25 went to principal."

"How would I know that? Your letter that originally notified us there was a problem (prior to my faxing you the cancelled check) didn't account for the funds you received when you cashed the Comcast check. Rather, it reflects and

190

claims: *nothing received towards November . . .*

"Well, we just found this in our research and, as far as the late fee, we will waive that. If this generates a 30-day late payment on Michael's credit, let us know and we'll take care of it," he said, as if that were so easily done. "As far as your question as to how we cashed the checks, we're large corporations and all those payments just get pushed through the system. We can't read them all."

"Well, that amazes me," I responded. "Are you saying that because you're a corporation you're allowed to cash checks that aren't made payable to you?" My ranting, however, seemed to get me nowhere. Instead, I paid the November payment over the telephone by giving him Michael's checking account number. The representative promised to credit the late fee and forward me a payment history schedule.

When I asked if I could start receiving monthly statements, he laughed out loud. "Do you honestly think we could send everybody a monthly statement?" he asked incredulously.

"Yes, if other companies do, why can't you?"

"It's not going to happen, but I will forward you the results of our investigation and if you have a problem with the credit report, let me know." Period, end of conversation!

As I sat and brewed over this all night, I couldn't wait to contact Comcast and hear what they had to say about cashing a check that was clearly made payable to our mortgage company, and learn their reasoning for not having the courtesy to notify us. I couldn't help but think that even though it was our *honest* mistake to mix up the mailing of the checks, we would have detected that mistake quickly had we received a monthly statement. In fact, I found that the cable company elected not to send us a statement that month. I could only surmise that was because now they had us paid in advance for months—sound familiar? There hadn't been enough time lapsed for us to have missed any non-delivery of the Comcast bill. It's funny how they can't find us to notify us that we overpaid our account by several hundreds of dollars, but they sure can find their customers when they don't make a payment.

I contacted Comcast as soon as I could. Their representative told me I could file a complaint with their corporate headquarters and provided me with their address. Michael had decided because they already had us paid in advance, let it be and just apprise them that we were not happy with how they handled the matter. Our position was that we should have received a phone call informing us they received our mortgage company check in error, knowing it could carry a huge impact because the money would never get in the hands of the mortgage company, causing us a late fee and blemishes on our credit. I compiled a letter and mailed it out, irritated but hoping naively that would end any more frustrations. The mortgage was paid, Comcast was notified of this fiasco and we were about to enjoy the Christmas holidays.

Florida, being considered a transient state, many of us can't always get home for the holidays and have no family nearby to celebrate with. We looked forward to enjoying the warm weather with an outdoor party around the pool surrounded with palm trees decorated in bright colors. It was going to make for a very festive night and everyone would get to see "Clark's" Christmas display he spent countless days perfecting. The day before our Christmas Eve party, Michael was outside setting up the yard while I was inside cooking a slew of different recipes to get ready for the party. We had Christmas carols playing in the background to heighten our Christmas spirit and were enjoying the preparations.

The phone rang late in the afternoon with a voice on the other end advising me he was calling from "Comcast Corporate" about my letter they received.

"We put a check in the mail to you today, but you better get to a cable office and pay your bill because now you are two months in the arrears."

"What?!," I exclaimed. "Why would you send me a check without deducting for the last couple of months from

192

the money you have been sitting on since October? Why would you make us try to find an open cable office on the eve of Christmas?"

"Isn't that what you wanted?" he asked snidely.

"No," I responded. "Nowhere in our letter does it say to send me back the money. It only apprises you of what in fact happened and our unhappiness with how you handled the situation. How can you tell me that you have had this money since October and now, on Christmas Eve, I must go pay two month's cable while the check you owe me is "*in the mail?*" That seems out-right malicious to me."

"Hold on," he abruptly said, "Let me go see if the mail has gone out yet." I sat on hold in amazement, my jaw open, wondering how they could do this to us and also in disbelief that over the holidays, it now appeared we were subject to losing our cable service. This was *after* they had been holding our funds for months, much like Shawmut did, as a type of interest-free loan. He came back on the line, "I caught it before the mail went out. Do you want us to apply it to your account?"

"Yes, I don't want to run around trying to find an open Comcast office to pay you money that you already have. Hold the entire amount and just leave our account paid in advance." When we hung up the phone, I relayed to Michael what the call was about.

"You know what, why don't we just check into a satellite service and drop them all together?" he proclaimed.

"Fine with me. I'll get on it after the holidays," I answered, feeling a huge sense of liberation. I wouldn't have to continue service with a company that seemed to care so little about the consequences we suffered as a result of their actions. It felt like we were taking a stand and it gave me great pleasure that I could soon call them and cancel our service.

When the holidays were over, I did just that. However, getting the remaining balance they owed us after cancelling our service with them in January, would take an additional two months. Luckily, this cable company and bank mix up was firmly behind me because I was immediately going to have to find space in my life for a return visit from my virtual tenant from hell—the June 2001 emergency room medical bill that I was sure was dead.

On January 3, of 2005, this monster reared up from the dead yet again. I came in the door that day just in time to hear the end of a message being left on my answering machine. "This is an urgent message for Denise Richardson. This is not a sales call." It couldn't be, I thought. The recording sounded so familiar—it was the same type of message I would hear when dealing with the many collection attempts made by NCO and Gold Key, regarding that 2001 paid medical bill. It couldn't possibly be same paid debt coming back at me again, could it?

As I replayed the entire message, I heard a stern message from Merchants Credit Guide relaying it was urgent and imperative that I call right away. I called and reached Mr. Hughes who explained that their client (NCO for MEDCLR) had "sold" a debt to them regarding a June 2001 medical bill. They purchased this debt as of December 2004 and he went on to insist I needed to pay this debt. I immediately told them that their "client" was notified many times, in writing, that this account was never delinquent and that Blue Cross/Blue Shield had not only paid it, but had spent hours with NCO providing them all the proof they needed. Just as the others, he too promised to review the matter, note my file and call back in a couple of days. *Off to research, to research, research . . .*

On January 6, 2005 I received their Notice of Collection in my mail. There it was—a letter from Merchants' Credit Guide Company demanding payment for their client, NCO Financial Systems, Inc:

"Please be advised, we represent the above client, NCO Financial Systems, Inc, for Medclr, Inc who has purchased your defaulted account from INPHYNET SOUTH BROWARD."

There was the same account number, same collection company and same creditors all attempting to collect on this same emergency room visit; balance due: $269.91.

I immediately contacted Merchant Credit Guide's office and spoke with a man who claimed his name was Mr. Sabba. He was not only demeaning, belligerent and rude but yelled at me through what sounded like clenched teeth, "Why *don't you just pay it?*"

I told him not only was it paid, they were notified of this and that under the FDCPA, they had violated my rights on numerous occasions.

"I will not pay something that has already paid. Why would I believe that my re-paying an already paid debt would suddenly stop your illegal attempts to collect on this non-existent debt? Further, what would make me believe your intimidating threats and harassing calls would then stop?"

I once again had to turn to Blue Cross/Blue Shield. I felt a sense of relief knowing they would be as outraged as I was that we were yet again being harassed for payment on a bill that (*they had knowledge of*) I didn't owe! I also felt a sense of humiliation every time I had to pick up that phone and call Blue Cross but just knowing they were there to turn to gave me that much needed support –I wasn't fighting them alone. I called Blue Cross and a rep named Jennifer spent an hour on the phone with me while she contacted both Merchants and Medclr. She faxed the proof this bill was paid - all over again. Interestingly, while on a call with Medclr, they told us not to send them any proof and they would not provide us the necessary address to forward our proof. She told us their policy was that we needed to send the information to the collection company *only* and once they received the documentation from the collection company –would they investigate our claims of dispute.

Jennifer, realizing they were being extremely rude and uncooperative, quickly replied,

"If I can send you the proof, then when you get the dispute from Merchants' you can easily handle it. The last time Ms. Richardson disputed this with the credit bureaus, their investigation results falsely indicated the account was reported and verified as accurate."

The Medclr representative insisted that she would contact the credit bureaus and remove the information but *only* once she ascertained it was in fact an error, and she insisted she *only* would do so after receiving the documentation from Merchants Credit Guide. Furthermore, she would not provide Blue Cross or me the fax number or address to send proof to them, again stating, "You can't send it to us–only to Merchants."

I relayed to Jennifer that I had just recently read that NCO was fined 1.5 million dollars for abusive or obviously flawed collection practices –at least according to a Consent Decree mandated by the FTC. I was going to seek what remedies I had under the consumer protection laws to stop this. Even though I was trying to avert the stress and high price (financially and emotionally) a court case would bring on, I feared, once again –I may find myself without a choice. Jennifer commented that she had documented the entire hour of frustrating attempts to clear this matter up and further told she was stunned that their harassment and continued attempts to collect on an obviously paid debt didn't appear to be stopping. She provided me with the phone number for BC/BS Third Party Liability.

"You might want to pass this information on to an attorney." She continued,

"You could then discuss getting copies of these well documented records. I wish you the best, Denise, and if there's anything *whatsoever* we can do to help, please call on us."

I was incredibly thankful for Blue Cross/Blue Shield's continued assistance in both documenting our many attempts to correct the problem and for their kindness and professionalism.

At that time I was utilizing a credit monitoring service that notified me the collection account was removed from my credit file. My credit score had gone back to the high 700's, which indicated excellent credit. All was well and it appeared that the hours of assistance from Blue Cross as well as Jennifer's unwavering patience and persistence had finally killed and buried the issue. That emergency room bill from June 2001 was now taken out of everyone's database and finally and forever buried and put to rest. I felt great relief that I didn't need to turn to the judicial system. The last thing I wanted was another unwanted lawsuit.

However, the relief I felt that my credit identity would soon be restored would turn out to be short lived. Sadly, this emergency room visit would not be the only (paid) zombie debt that would yet again affect my credit identity.

True to the past, shortly after successfully erasing the June 2001 emergency room debt from my credit report, in April of 2005, another collection notice appeared in my mailbox. This time, it wasn't for the same June 2001 visit. Rather, this notice was an attempt to collect a so-called balance due from *a December 2000* hospital visit. This time they were demanding $660.

The past had taught me the need to save all receipts including all my medical bill receipts. I specifically remembered this particular visit to the emergency room as it was shortly after moving to Florida. The Saturday afternoon I received my latest collection notice in the mail, I spent the entire afternoon going through boxes of receipts –praying I would find the necessary proof that could, just like the 2001 bill, prove I didn't owe this bill either. Sure enough, I did. I found my co-pay receipts and the receipt from the hospital that indicated "balance paid in full" and further noted that Blue Cross had paid the bill in its *entirety.*

Armed with this information, I contacted the collection company. I asked them why, after all these years, they were trying to collect on a bill that was paid 5 years ago. Their explanation was a response I had never heard before –it was quite remarkable.

"Well, you're right," they said.

"*It was paid,* however, Blue Cross accessed our account in March of this year and deducted this amount. Apparently, they decided to reject payment after all these years and you need to pay it. I don't know why you didn't receive notice and don't know why they did this, but they did. You'll have to take that up with them."

"WHAT!" I didn't for one minute believe them. I had been dealing with Blue Cross for many years and found them helpful and professional. They always went above and beyond what should be expected of them and I couldn't bring myself to believe they would arbitrarily decide to rescind payment of a bill from December 2000 and –not notify me! I didn't trust the explanation and contacted Blue Cross immediately to find out if the collection company was telling me the truth.

"Can I place you on hold, Denise, while I check into this?" the BC/BS shield representative, Shawn, asked. "Your file shows we did not retract or rescind our initial payment. I do need to speak to my supervisor about this."

"Of course,"

"Talk to whomever you need—I'm happy to hold."

Soon, Shawn came back on the line and said they needed all the contact information of the collection company that claimed Blue Cross rescinded their payment and essentially took the money back. He assured me they had not revoked the funds and, through their research, it appeared that this particular collection company or the hospital was doing something they refer to in the industry as "balance billing."

He explained that when a hospital agrees to be a Blue Cross provider, they also agree to accept the pre-determined lesser payment for the specified services paid by Blue Cross. The hospitals (providers) acknowledge it is good business because they make up for any reduction in payments through the mass volume of patients they receive by simply being a Blue Cross provider. Balance billing occurs when a hospital (provider) bills the patient in an attempt to collect money that they agreed they were not entitled to. Shawn went on to explain "I'm bumping this complaint up to our legal department because "balance billing" is not acceptable and in breach their contract with Blue Cross."

While I had never heard of "balance billing" before

my own skirmish, it proves that you need to recognize that you just may not be responsible for particular bills that end up in your mailbox and more importantly, never trust a collection company that insists you owe a debt –without obtaining the proof that you do! Always check with your insurer to ascertain if they have paid the bill or if you are, in fact, even accountable for the amount the hospital is trying to collect. It could just be an attempted "balance billing," where the hospital or collection company is trying to collect funds they are not entitled to.

Shawn collected all the pertinent information and promised to contact the collection agency, making sure I received confirmation this collection would disappear. After the necessary disputes were filed and a few more phone calls placed, two months later I finally received a letter from the collection company confirming they had sent a request to removed the erroneous medical bill from my credit file. Then I finally received confirmation from the credit bureaus that the information was removed from my report.

Their letter stated in part: *"We have received authorization from the facility to retract/delete our collection entry from your credit file."*

Would it be this easy? Would this 2000 collection attempt stay dead? Could I finally expect to get the interest rates and insurance premiums that my accurate credit rating deserved?

Not quite...

Just like the movie villain who pops up yet one more time to threaten his victim before finally dying, in March of 2006, I walked into the house and quite nonchalantly pressed the button to hear my messages. There was a message on my answering machine that sounded so eerily familiar.

"This is an urgent message for Denise Richardson, this is not a sales call, you must call us at 800-blah-blah-blah." The message was left by the law firm of Riddle & Associates *"on behalf of our client—NCO"*.

I contacted Riddle & Associates. "On February, 2006, we purchased a debt you owe to our client NCO/Medclr."

"Well, you once again purchased a debt that doesn't exist! I would like to speak to the attorney in charge of this account from the law firm you represent."

"I can't let you speak to him directly but you can have your attorney call 800-blah-blah and speak to him."

"Why haven't I received a notice of this collection attempt in the mail as the law mandates?"

They relayed that they sent notice –but to my previous address –where I hadn't lived in nearly two years. He asked for my current address so he could then forward me a letter. "Yes, please do send me the letter so I can dispute it! Have you ever heard of the FDCPA or the FCRA?"

A few days later, I received their "Demand for Payment" letter which stated:

Our Client: NCO Financial Systems
Account Purchaser: MedCLR, Inc
Original Creditor: Inphynet South
    Broward, Inc.

Our law firm has been retained to collect the total amount due of $223.00.

Strangely, or not so strangely, I noticed that even though the letterhead said Riddle & Associates, PC, Attorneys and Counselors at law, the letter went on to state: "For additional information concerning our privacy policy, you may write us, in care of **our servicer at: NCO Financial Systems,** Inc. P.O. Box 8547, Philadelphia, PA." There was that same old Post Office Box that was referred to in all of my prior credit reports and on each of my prior collection notices.

I disputed this debt again and once again contacted Blue Cross. Then the annoying phone calls began. A particular annoying call came in one early Sunday morning at 9:08 am. It was a pre-recorded message alerting me of another "urgent message for Denise Richardson". I returned the call immediately. I could feel my heart racing as I dialed the number and knew I was seething with anger ready to disperse it out on whoever answered the call. But instead of getting a person I received their voice mail telling me their offices were closed on Sundays! How is it okay that they can call consumers and leave "urgent" pre-recorded messages, while all the while...they have the day off!

After NCO received my most recent dispute forwarded to them, their latest response arrived in the mail and read in part;

> "...Thank you for your recent inquiry. This is an attempt to collect a debt... Please be advised we have contacted the credit bureaus with which we do business with our request to delete our listing... However, NCO Financial Systems, Inc. cannot affect a change to how any other company or entity may have listed the account...."

Now that is just bull! Each time this erroneous data was furnished to the credit bureaus, **NCO** was the furnisher. However, the credit report reflected the furnisher as Medclr, deliberately misleading and making it nearly impossible to correct. I learned the address for Medclr was the same as that of NCO because every credit report referred me to that address for further information. I remembered the first time I tried to contact Medclr. It was impossible—I kept getting a collection company and didn't know why.

I knew I was being tossed about in their deliberate circle of deceit designed to confuse the consumer and escape liability. How is a consumer to know *who is whom* when they hide behind different corporate names? Plus NCO's stance that they *"cannot affect change to how any other company lists this account"* is not only ludicrous but also clearly demonstrates their attempt to protect themselves from any future accountability or *knowingly* wrongdoing. This is a portion of a press release found on NCO's website;

Glen Falls, NY and Baltimore, MD, *August 18, 2003* - **MEDCLR,** A Marlin Company LLC, one of the leading providers of after collection solutions for hospital, medical services and emergency room physician companies in the country, and **joint venture partner NCO Portfolio Management,** Inc. (Nasdaq: NCPM), a leading purchaser and manager of delinquent accounts receivable, announced today that they signed an agreement with American Medical Response, Inc. (AMR), one of the nation's largest providers of medical transportation, to buy, at a discount, the delinquent accounts receivable of AMR with a face value of $500 million.

Their latest letter to me didn't include an apology, nor explanation or remorse. They simply signed it "Very Truly Yours." With this in mind, I hope my story and the others contained in this book provides you with the necessary information you need to ensure your credit identity is in fact –very truly yours.

Chapter Lesson: Will Your Complaints Be Heard?

If you think my case is unique, trust me –it most definitely is not. It's systemic within the collection industry. Here are a couple of findings regarding NCOs' procedures

May 13, 2004 posted on the Federal Trade Commission's Web site: www.ftc.gov

NCO Group to Pay Largest FCRA Civil Penalty to Date

One of the nation's largest debt-collection firms will pay $1.5 million to settle Federal

Trade Commission charges that it violated the Fair Credit Reporting Act (FCRA) by reporting inaccurate information about consumer accounts to credit bureaus. The civil penalty against Pennsylvania-based NCO Group, Inc. is the largest civil penalty ever obtained in a FCRA case.

According to the FTC's complaint, defendants NCO Group, Inc.; NCO Financial Systems, Inc.; and NCO Portfolio Management, Inc. violated Section 623(a)(5) of the FCRA, which specifies that any entity that reports information to credit bureaus about a delinquent consumer account that has been placed for collection or written off must report the actual month and year the account first became delinquent. In turn, this date is used by the credit bureaus to measure the maximum seven-year reporting period the FCRA mandates. The provision helps to ensure that outdated debts–debts that are beyond this seven-year reporting period–do not appear on a consumer's credit report. Violations of this provision of the FCRA are subject to civil penalties of $2,500 per violation.

The FTC charges that NCO reported accounts using later-than-actual delinquency dates. Reporting later-than-actual dates may cause negative information to remain in a consumer's credit file beyond the seven-year reporting period permitted by the FCRA. When this occurs, consumers' credit scores are lowered, possibly resulting in a credit rejection or their having to pay a higher interest rate.

The proposed consent decree orders the defendants to pay civil penalties of $1.5 million and permanently bars them from reporting later-than-actual delinquency dates to credit bureaus in the future. Additionally, NCO is required to implement a program to monitor all complaints received to ensure that reporting errors are corrected quickly. The consent agreement also contains standard recordkeeping and other requirements to assist the FTC in monitoring the defendant's compliance.

NOTE: The Commission files a complaint when it has "reason to believe" that the law has been or is being violated, and it appears to the Commission that a proceeding is in the public interest. The complaint is not a finding or ruling that the defendant has actually violated the law. NOTE: This stipulated final order is for settlement purposes only and does not constitute an admission by the defendant of a law violation. A stipulated final order requires approval by the court and has the force of law when signed by the judge."

It appears, however, that whatever recordkeeping they may or may not have implemented as the FTC required, hasn't worked. Here is a notice of a settlement with the Attorney General of Pennsylvania:

January 27, 2006:

Pennsylvania Attorney General Corbett
announces settlement agreement with PA
based debt collector NCO Financial Systems

HARRISBURG – Attorney General Tom Corbett today announced that a settlement has been reached with Pennsylvania based NCO Financial Systems Inc., a national debt collection agency, following an investigation into in excess of 800 consumer complaints lodged with the Attorney General's Bureau of Consumer Protection against NCO Financial since November 2003.

Corbett said NCO Financial, headquartered at 507 Prudential Road, Horsham, entered into an agreement, known as an Assurance of Voluntary Compliance, with the Attorney General's Office for alleged violations of the state's Consumer Protection Law and Fair Credit Extension Uniformity Act, and the Federal Fair Debt Collection Practices Act.

Corbett said that the alleged violations included engaging in or using unfair or deceptive debt collection acts and/or practices, and engaging in or using false, deceptive, or misleading representations or means in connection with the collection of debts.

Corbett said that many consumer complaints involved claims that NCO Financial improperly contacted consumers at their place of employment, or called at unusual times or at times NCO Financial knew, or should have known, were inconvenient to the consumer, such as calling consumers before 8 a.m. and/or after 9 p.m.

Other consumer complaints alleged that representatives of NCO Financial used obscene or profane language and engaged in conduct to threaten, annoy, abuse, or harass consumers.

Corbett said there were also allegations that NCO Financial continued to communicate with consumers after the consumer had notified them in writing that the debt was in dispute or that the consumer wished the debt collector to stop calling.

"Many consumers were very upset after they had received abusive or threatening calls from NCO Financial, in some instances even after the consumer had unsuccessfully tried to tell them that they did not owe the debt," Corbett said. "In many cases, these calls did not stop until the Attorney General's Bureau of Consumer Protection got involved."

Under the terms of the Assurance, NCO Financial denies the Commonwealth's allegations and agrees to:

- Adopt and implement policies and procedures reasonably necessary to ensure that its representatives are properly trained and are otherwise performing their duties in compliance with all applicable laws.

- Adhere to a policy of disciplining, up to and including the termination of, representatives that have not complied with the requirements of the Assurance and all applicable laws.

- Sufficiently monitor independent contractors and when it learns that any independent contractor is acting in violation of the requirements of the Assurance, immediately take action to enforce its contractual rights, up to and including termination of any independent contractor.

- Adopt and implement compliance monitoring policies and procedures, under which NCO Financial's supervisors and managers of call centers must spend a portion of their work time monitoring by any lawful means their representatives to ensure compliance with applicable laws and company policy.

- Pay to the Commonwealth the sum of $300,000 as costs of investigation and/or for future public protection purposes.

Note: According to a recent Boston, MA news station investigation, the Massachusetts Attorney General's office opened an investigation of complaints against NCO's collection practices.

Epilogue

Questions of my *identity* have been a prevalent theme throughout my life. Never knowing my biological father meant being ignorant of my heritage, my medical history and one half of myself and my family. Those are things I grew to live with over time. Yes, there were periods of pain involved with my obvious personal identity struggles but nothing that compared with the struggle to regain and keep my credit identity.

This battle was tortuous and complex, and stressed every facet of my life to the near breaking point. If some good can come from my sharing this story, then perhaps my journey had reason –and value. I know that my strong desire to help others, coupled with my experiences, made this book a personal necessity. I make no apologies to those that don't like my truthfulness and so-called *activism.* I hope you understand that my story is not unique—that description is simply a defensive mechanism the credit industry uses to dismiss anyone who dares to tell their story. It's important to humanize and expose the steep price an innocent consumer pays when faced with inaccurate credit, if we really want to repair the current system, educate others and open avenues for change.

I must believe that the events of the past 15 years ensued for a purpose and were a pre-destined path. I can't help but wonder what my life *would've, could've, and should've* been like if I hadn't lived this twisted tale. What I do know, is that this book would never have been written if my story could have ended after the Federal case. But it obviously didn't and after much encouragement to tell my story –to help shed light on the issues I've raised, I can't help but hope that my story produces at least a small degree of change for others. That then, would prove for certain that *everything does happen for a reason.* We just need to find the reason.

So, what did I learn from my exhaustive experiences? What do I think I did right and what could I have done better? I'm often asked, if I had a chance to turn back the hands of time and relive the events that triggered the dominos to fall 15 years ago, would I handle things differently? You bet. Absolutely. I know I learned quite a bit through trial and error. There were a lot of errors, some of which greatly contributed to the destruction of my marriage as well as the emotional and psychological scars I carry today. From what I have seen, this is very common, so it warrants the telling. Life altering events can and do either bring families together or shred them apart. Having the ability to see with perfect hindsight, I can clearly differentiate between the bumps in the road that one can get over and the deep sinkholes one can fall into if unaware of their existence. Though this book includes chapter lessons on the system itself, I'd like to share a few personal insights that I hope will steer you away from a fall into one of those bottomless sinkholes.

A large part of the battle for your credit identity can appear to begin as a simple problem that with a small amount of perseverance—a letter or two or maybe a quick phone call—can be easily corrected. Don't be fooled! Hours swiftly turn into days and days into weeks and weeks into months. Before you know it, a year passes and you finally realize –there is no quick fix. My best advice to anyone facing this situation would be to pay close attention to your personal life –what is going on around you. Do not be drawn so far into the battle that you lose sight of the rest of your life and what is truly important. If one person in the family is more skilled in writing dispute letters, making phone calls, contacting enforcement agencies and other such things—as I was—do it, but don't go it alone. Share every letter, phone call and frustration with your partner from the start. The reason is simple. If you don't start at the beginning you will soon find it too overwhelming to easily bring your family up to speed and you could wake up to realize they've moved on without you.

As my life and credit errors grew out of control, I found my husband had little interest in what I was doing to clear up the problem because he didn't have to worry-I was handling everything. His life continued happily without any awareness of how out of control the situation had become and how much stress was involved. The massive intrusions had grown so large and complex that I didn't feel as though I had the strength to get his attention or even the ability to articulate how monstrous this burden had become. I came to believe it was <u>my</u> problem and <u>my</u> job to fix everything. When I needed support, I didn't turn to him –he wasn't there for me to turn to. I turned to other victims. I am not saying that turning to other victims was something I did wrong— rather, that was one thing I did right. The online consumer forums and consumer letters were a much needed source of strength and support and let me know I wasn't alone. Unfortunately, my husband should have been sitting right there next to me, reading those letters to truly understand the consequences paid by innocent families.

The effects of their actions changes people – irrevocably. There is no way back to the old "you" that was stolen with your identity.

Turning to each other *and* other victims or advocates for mutual support is crucial during any hardship. That's why support groups were born and function as a necessary source of strength when troubles enter our lives. This is no different. When you turn to other victims, *don't turn away from your loved ones.* Take them on that that not-so-merry-go-round ride with you. Remember: hardships can either break down relationships or build them stronger. It's imperative that you don't turn away from help and support. Instead, run to it.

Another important lesson I learned, albeit a bit too late, is to contact the right person at the company you are dealing with when trying to find accountability for, and relief from your particular problem. There is a very easy way to find out who the President or CEO is in most large companies. Go to your browser and type in the name of the company you are searching for and the words "financial profile" (including the quotation marks). You are looking for the Yahoo! financial profile, which is powered by Hoovers. This page will provide you with the names of officers in the company, including phone and fax numbers. Once you have this information, you can fax a letter to, or call the President or CEO of the company. I believe most CEO's would like to be informed of these types of problems and any possible breakdown of their system, before it reaches the courtroom doors. If not, this gives you the option, if worse comes to worst, to notify the particular officer that you may be forced to initiate legal action against the company *and* him/her – personally, since you have now made that officer aware of the situation.

Remember, employees often view companies in the way that citizens view their government, thinking, "It's not my money." When an officer of a company understands that he may be named in a lawsuit, that realization can often exert enough pressure to produce the kind of corrections you are looking for. Remember when dealing with a corporation *they* rarely follow society's rule to take responsibility, admit mistakes or accept liability for any wrongdoing. It creates a quagmire. Corporations have a fiduciary duty to their stockholders to maximize company profits, placing corporate interests directly at odds with consumer interests. Even so, I would venture to say that were a lawsuit to affect their personal lives and their personal finances, they may be more amenable to correcting the problem rather than risking being held personally liable.

Looking back on my experiences, I learned a lot about the legal system. I learned if you want to win the game, you must know the rules. In hindsight, some of my decisions may not have been the best. My federal suit had five defendants with Fleet being the party assigned the highest culpability. By agreeing to settle with them, and releasing them from my lawsuit, I essentially gave a gift to the remaining defendants. After a plaintiff settles with the leading defendant, the court views the funds received from the plaintiff as compensation based on the percentage of blame assigned to that (settled) defendant. This ultimately left me with a greater degree of difficulty in proving the damages attributed to each remaining defendant. It placed a heavier burden on my attorneys as we tried to establish the defendants' individual percentage of culpability. In Equifax's case, they held on until they were the last party standing—I believe that was their strategy. In doing so, they claimed no blame and furthermore asserted, among other things, that I had already been compensated for my losses by the settled defendants. Besides this, it becomes easy for a holdout defendant to use the trial tactic of pointing to the empty chairs and agreeing that the plaintiff was injured—by the missing defendants, who already paid. I would advise anyone in the same circumstances to carefully consider the benefits of keeping the case together or settling. Consult with an experienced attorney before agreeing to *any* settlement.

Regarding legal assistance, my experience would lead me to advise you that you need to contact the right attorney <u>as soon as you have documented your complaints</u>. Don't waste time or wait years as I did, falsely believing in their countless promises to correct the problems. An inexperienced attorney can prove costly. A well-prepared attorney can come to your aid when consumer protection laws are twisted and used against you. They can guide you through the loopholes contained in these statutes and help to stop the creditors and the CRAs from sliding out of the loopholes while trying to escape accountability.

Make sure you find an experience litigator (unlike Betty) that is experienced and well-versed in the array of consumer protection Acts out there, such as the Fair Credit Reporting Act, Fair and Accurate Credit Transaction Act, Fair Debt Collection Practices Act, Equal Credit Opportunity Act, Truth in Lending Act, etc. Lastly, you must **act** to protect yourself and create your own plan of action to prevent a battle like mine from invading your life. Just remember the acronym below;

ACT

Account for all loan payments and verify they are **applied accurately**; review your credit file and **always be aware** of **adverse action** that may have been taken against you based on inaccurate information;

Contact the right person—the **correct attorney** or law firm, the correct agencies— and always send **certified mail**; Maintain **copious notes** in a journal or day book of every person you spoke with, every penny spent and every hour you devoted to correcting the problem;

Turn to others for support and strength— *including* your loved ones. Paint a picture— **tell your story** to the media, your Legislators and consumer groups. Get the **truth** out there!

Following these guidelines can help you guard your credit, reduce your odds of becoming a victim and lessen the degree your life is impacted if your credit becomes an issue.

Remember: there is power in numbers –especially those *three digits that define your credit identity*. Consumers and their advocates can also find power in numbers by combining their voices and their efforts to fight for a real change.

Reach out to the consumer community. Speak out and tell your story. It can be cathartic and provide inspiration for others to do the same. What better way to show the need for change than painting a human face on the true effects caused by broken systems and weak laws?

My lengthy credit identity battles motivated me to tell my story to both encourage others to speak out and to expose the need for stronger consumer protection laws. As it stands now –our laws appear to be the best laws money can buy. Please, contact your Legislators by phone or mail and let them know we need laws that money can't buy!

We also need monthly statements to verify how and if our payments are applied! Remember, just because you may be receiving a monthly statement on your current mortgage, your mortgage could be sold, you may purchase another home or refinance and soon you may find you are forced to blindly trust where you money is going.

If you're paying additional principal payments as I did, make sure you **verify** the payments are applied accurately and allocated as a reduction to the principal balance –and not applied towards *future* payments. (Remember; auto payments, student loan payments and escrow accounts are also vulnerable to errors)

If you want to help make a difference, tell your story or sign my petition supporting the need for monthly statements –please visit givemebackmycredit.com or guardmycreditfile.org –and let me know.

They often say *what you don't know –won't hurt you.* I've learned the hard way *–they* are dead wrong. You need to know what is contained in your credit file, how your payments are being applied and what your rights are.

It's what *you don't know that will hurt you...*believe me, I know.

About the Author

Denise Richardson his been an avid consumer advocate for fifteen years working steadfast in her resolve to bring greater transparency to the credit industry and to improve the way that consumers are treated by creditors and the credit reporting agencies.

She is a contributing writer for *guardmycredifile.org* and holds a seat on the board of Directors of American Consumer Credit Education Support Services (ACCESS).

Denise was born and raised in Vermont before becoming a long time resident of Greenfield, Massachusetts. Currently residing in Hollywood, Florida she encourages consumers to contact her at *givemebackmycredit.com* if interested in helping to make a difference for others.

Printed in the United States
74637LV00002B/127